Cambridge Elements ≡

Elements in Ethics
edited by
Ben Eggleston
University of Kansas
Dale E. Miller
Old Dominion University, Virginia

PRIORITARIANISM

Richard J. Arneson
University of California

CAMBRIDGE
UNIVERSITY PRESS

University Printing House, Cambridge CB2 8BS, United Kingdom

One Liberty Plaza, 20th Floor, New York, NY 10006, USA

477 Williamstown Road, Port Melbourne, VIC 3207, Australia

314–321, 3rd Floor, Plot 3, Splendor Forum, Jasola District Centre,
New Delhi – 110025, India

103 Penang Road, #05–06/07, Visioncrest Commercial, Singapore 238467

Cambridge University Press is part of the University of Cambridge.

It furthers the University's mission by disseminating knowledge in the pursuit of
education, learning, and research at the highest international levels of excellence.

www.cambridge.org
Information on this title: www.cambridge.org/9781108730693
DOI: 10.1017/9781108582865

First published 2022

A catalogue record for this publication is available from the British Library.

ISBN 978-1-108-73069-3 Paperback
ISSN 2516-4031 (online)
ISSN 2516-4023 (print)

Prioritarianism

Elements in Ethics

DOI: 10.1017/9781108582865
First published online: May 2022

Richard J. Arneson
University of California

Author for correspondence: Richard J. Arneson, rarneson@ucsd.edu

Abstract: Prioritarianism holds that improvements in someone's life (gains in well-being) are morally more valuable, the worse off the person would otherwise be. The doctrine is impartial, holding that a gain in one person's life counts exactly the same as an identical gain in the life of anyone equally well-off. If we have some duty of beneficence to make the world better, prioritarianism specifies the content of the duty. Unlike the utilitarian, the prioritarian holds that we should not only seek to increase human well-being but also distribute it fairly across persons by tilting in favor of the worse off. A variant version adds that we should also give priority to the morally deserving – to saints over scoundrels. The view is a standard for right choice of individual actions and public policies, offering a distinctive alternative to utilitarianism (maximize total well-being), sufficiency (make everyone's condition good enough), and egalitarianism (make everyone's condition the same).

Keywords: well-being, equality, utilitarianism, public policy, normative political theory

ISBNs: 9781108730693 (PB), 9781108582865 (OC)
ISSNs: 2516-4031 (online), 2516-4023 (print)

Contents

1 The Priority Idea   1

2 Some Clarifications and Further Questions   16

3 Priority for the Deserving   26

4 Utilitarianism, Sufficiency, and Leximin   41

5 Egalitarianism versus Prioritarianism   53

6 Conclusion   69

   References   70

1 The Priority Idea

1.1 Dolores and Felicity

Dolores has had a rough life. Very rough. She has been homeless, on and off, for much of her adult life. She has been mentally ill since adolescence, and her illness makes her charmless and grasping, so she does not attract much sympathy from those who observe her plight. Family members help her occasionally but find helping her unrewarding, so they don't do anywhere nearly as much for her as they know they should. She has bounced in and out of halfway houses and government-supplied apartments for the disabled, always violating whatever rules are in force and chafing at restrictions on her freedom. She prizes her freedom but lacks the capacity to use it to her advantage in any way. She has lived on a meager income grant for disabled individuals. She has few resources, but even worse, very little capacity to transform whatever resources she has into well-being.[1]

In contrast, consider Felicity. She has been extremely fortunate in her life and is looking forward to a happy old age. She has been enormously successful in business, amassing not only stupendous wealth but also great creative achievements of the sort any of us, in sensible moods, would want for ourselves. She has been blessed in family life and friendship, and when not working or engaged productively with family and friends, plays hard and with zest.

Felicity has already reached a very high level of lifetime well-being and is headed to further peaks beyond that ridgeline. As already mentioned, she has secure and stable command of immense resources that she can use for her own benefit. Moreover, part of her charm and good fortune is that she has immense capacity to turn resources into personal fulfillment (well-being or welfare). Give her a new yacht, she beams and will gain great benefit from this change in her life, notwithstanding the fact that she already owns around 100 magnificent yachts.

Now imagine you happen to face a rare opportunity, at a small cost to yourself, to do a significant good turn for one of two people ready at hand – as it happens, to either Dolores or Felicity. You can give one or the other a large bowl of delicious gelato that will otherwise go to waste. You have no other viable alternatives. There are no further complexities or nuances in the situation. Nobody will notice what you choose or what follows. There will be no significant long-term or indirect effects of giving the ice cream to Felicity or alternatively to Dolores. Although Felicity has recently had some fine ice cream, she would, being Felicity, gain a significant well-being boost

---

[1] The description of Dolores applies to a real person. ("Dolores" is not her real name.)

from getting this ice-cream gift from you. Dolores would get some benefit, but smaller. She has bad teeth, which tingle with something sweet in her mouth, diminishing the enjoyment she gets from the ice cream. She will for sure drop the bowl or get distracted and only consume a fraction of what you give her. Your action in giving the ice cream to one or the other will give rise to no effects except to bring about a one-unit enjoyment and well-being gain for Dolores, if you give it to her, or to bring about a three-unit enjoyment and well-being gain for Felicity, if you give it to her. To put the numbers in perspective, assume Felicity's lifetime well-being without this benefit will be 10,000 and Dolores's 800. What should you do?

1.2 Some Clarifications and a Statement of the Priority View

I admit this is a far-fetched and trivial scenario, but bear with me. I'm just making a point. Notice first of all that the influential and prominent doctrine called *utilitarianism*, as a criterion of morally right action, will definitely yield the judgment that you ought to give the ice cream to Felicity, not Dolores. Utilitarianism says, one ought always to do whatever would bring about the best reachable outcome, and in this small decision problem, the difference your action will make is, all things considered, either to bring about a one-unit well-being gain or alternatively a three-unit gain. Utilitarianism says you should do what will bring about the greater gain and thereby the better outcome. Utilitarianism tells us that in deciding what to do, from a moral perspective, one ought to pay no heed to the distribution of well-being gains across persons, just the sum total.

Some take this distribution-free character to be a black mark against utilitarianism. However, according to many more who have considered utilitarianism, the fact that it turns a blind eye to issues of distribution is among the least of its defects. These further supposed defects are beyond the topic of this Element, which focuses on fair distribution issues. Two fair distribution issues loom large. One comes out in the Dolores and Felicity parable: we should be maximizing, not the sum of well-being, but a transformation of this well-being sum that gives priority to gains for those who are worse off. Utilitarianism has built into it no special solicitude for the wretched of the Earth, and this is a defect. The utilitarian response to this demand to favor the badly off is discussed in Section 4.

The second big distributional concern starts with the thought that striving hard, maybe against the grain of your given personality proclivities, to be decent and nice to other people increases the moral value of gaining a boost in well-being for you or preventing a loss. What has been described as the unblinking accountant's eye of the utilitarian counts a same-sized welfare benefit going to either a deserving or an undeserving person as having in itself exactly the same moral value. The opposed view is that we should give priority to the deserving. More on this second issue in Section 3.

A preliminary point to notice is that although the Dolores and Felicity example posed is stylized and simple, in broad outline, this type of decision problem often recurs and, described in some ways, is ubiquitous. People who are poor by wealth and income measures tend to be worse off than others in significant quality of life. It may be true, as they say, that the best things in life are free, but those best things tend to have prerequisites that are not free, rather costly. Also, another feature of the Felicity–Dolores example shows up often: people who are imprudent, or in some other way are poor transformers of resources into well-being gains for themselves, will tend to be worse off than others even if their access to resources is similar to the access of those who are better transformers. Of course, huge numbers of people suffer cruel oppression. But the thing about oppression is, even if you are very stalwart, it grinds you down and tends to render your quality of life Dolores-like.

Another complication in framing the Felicity–Dolores beneficence problem has already been noted two paragraphs back: you might wonder if Felicity has made herself into a person who is an efficient transformer of resources into well-being and made herself into a reasonable, prudent person and should get moral credit for those character improvements. You might incline to believe Felicity is especially deserving, and on this ground is a more apt recipient of beneficence than Dolores. You might also wonder how Dolores came to be in steady peril. Maybe she is partly to blame for the fact that she has so evidently traipsed down the wrong path. Thinking along these lines starts to look like an excuse for not helping and for not worrying much about how the background causes of social misery might be fixed.

To simplify things, let us set this issue to the side, for now. As already mentioned, we return to issues of deservingness, moral worth, blameworthiness, and personal responsibility in Section 3. To proceed, just assume that Felicity is far better off than Dolores through no merit of Felicity and through no fault of Dolores.

A final preliminary clarification, before venturing a verdict on the decision problem, whether to help Felicity or Dolores, is that to focus on the issue at hand, we should explicitly state that you do not have some prior duty to do something else with the resources you are thinking of giving to one of these two individuals. It's yours to hand out. To put it cautiously, if there are any deontic moral duties or moral rights that register at the fundamental level of moral principle, they do not have any application to this example. We put it cautiously because not everyone accepts such deontic constraints, and perhaps, at the fundamental moral level, no one should.

With this stage-setting in place, I myself have a strong intuition to the effect that you ought to offer the bowl of gelato to Dolores, not Felicity. Here I can only appeal to the reader's intuition about the issue, once it is clearly posed. Sure, Felicity will get more out of it. The good at stake here is enjoyment, and we stipulate that Felicity would get more enjoyment from eating the ice cream than would Dolores. However, the thought is that given how badly off Dolores is in lifetime terms, it is morally more important, morally better to provide the benefit to her rather than to Felicity. It is good for either of them to get the ice cream, given either would enjoy it, and the fact that Felicity would enjoy it more is a reason to give it to her, but this reason is outweighed by a countervailing reason: a well-being increase for a person matters more, the worse off the person would otherwise be over the course of her life. A slightly misleading shorthand slogan expressing this claim is that benefits matter more; the worse off the person is who gets the benefits.

In other words, in considering who should be the recipient of your benefi-cence, you should give priority to the worse off. This is the basic claim of the moral doctrine that has come to be known as prioritarianism or the priority view.

1.3 Equality or Priority?

In a famous essay on "Equality," Thomas Nagel describes an example similar to our Felicity–Dolores example (Nagel 1979). Nagel imagines a parent who is contemplating a family move that would have differential effects on her two children. One child has a severe physical disability, so his life prospects are significantly worse than those of his well-functioning sibling. We can suppose that by any plausible measure of individual well-being, the able child is heading for greater lifetime well-being than the disabled child will reach. The family faces a stark choice: either move to a city, enabling the handicapped child to get special medical treatment, or move to a suburb, lacking access to ready special care for this child but clearly providing better opportunities for the flourishing of the already well-functioning child. Nagel adds this twist: the able child will gain more benefit from the move to the suburb than the disabled child would gain from the move to the city. Assume we must choose one or the other of these two options. Assume also that there are no other reasons, except for the effects on the children's welfare, that favor either move.

In both the Dolores–Felicity example and Nagel's example, the numbers matter. If the difference between the gain the able child would get from the suburb choice and the gain the disabled child would obtain from the city choice were very slight, the reason to favor the disabled child would increase. If the difference between how well-off the able child will be apart from this choice and how well-off the disabled child will be is very small, the reason to favor the disabled child would diminish.

Nagel asserts that there would be an egalitarian reason to make the choice that favors the disabled child. This assertion might be read as another way of saying there is a prioritarian reason to favor the disabled child. That is to say, the fact that the one child is very badly off, in absolute terms, gives an extra moral reason to aid him if we can.

But a more straightforward way to interpret Nagel's claim is to recognize it makes an ineliminably comparative claim: the fact that the one child is far worse off than the other is what generates a moral reason to opt for the city move. We should at least, to some extent, be equalizing the outcomes or expectable outcomes of people.

Are these two different notions or really the same idea in different guise? In a remarkable essay, delivered as the Lindley Lecture at the University of Kansas, Derek Parfit (1995) clarified for philosophers the distinction between equality and priority. Priority says, a benefit obtained for a person is in itself morally more valuable, the worse off in absolute terms the person would otherwise be. Equality says, it is intrinsically morally valuable to bring it about that different people's condition is the same or closer to the same. So stated, the two views are views about the moral assessment of outcomes. They also become two views about what we morally ought to do if we add that, for the prioritarian, we ought to bring about outcomes in which the sum of people's benefits adjusted by each one's prioritarian weight, and for the egalitarian, we ought to bring about outcomes in which people's condition is the same or closer to the same.

Parfit explains the distinction between equality and priority in these words:

> It may help to use this analogy. People at higher altitudes find it harder to breathe. Is this because they are higher up than other people? In one sense, yes. But they would find it just as hard to breathe even if there were no other people who were lower down. In the same way, on the Priority View, benefits to the worse-off matter more, but that is only because these people are at a lower *absolute* level. It is irrelevant that these people are worse off *than others*. Benefits to them would matter just as much even if there *were* no others who were better off (Parfit 1995, 23).

For now, we simply acknowledge that having an inclination to believe that one ought to give the gelato to Dolores, not Felicity, and an inclination to believe that the parent ought to move to the city, not the country does not necessarily indicate an inclination to believe the priority view is correct. The same judgments have alternative rationales. One is egalitarian.

Another possible rationale is sufficientarian (Frankfurt 1988; Crisp 2003; Benbaji 2005, 2006). Sufficiency says that what matters is that everyone has enough. In a slogan, what matters morally in itself is not that some people have more or less than others but rather that some do not have enough – they face excessively low well-being prospects. The prospects in question could be deemed to be prospects for the moment just ahead, or a stretch of future time, or the whole future course of the person's life, or the person's entire lifetime from birth to death. These same options for ranking are open for priority and equality as well.

Sufficiency, when advanced as a view about what is morally right and wrong, says that what each of us owes others is that they have enough and as a view about social justice says that the imperative of justice is to institute social arrangements that provide enough to each and every person. Applied to the Dolores and Felicity decision problem, the sufficiency advocate will say that on its natural interpretation, Felicity is above sufficiency and Dolores is below, and this is the crucial feature that determines what would be right to do in this case. One ought to help Dolores, not Felicity, and one ought to do so because she alone is below the sufficiency threshold, not to bring the distribution of well-being closer to equality, and not on the basis that Dolores is worse off. If we revise the example so that the well-being gap between the two potential beneficiaries of one's choice is the same, but both individuals are above sufficiency, this moral imperative to favor Dolores disappears.

Yet another alternative explanation of at least some moral judgments resembling priority is negatively weighted utilitarianism (NWU). This is a version of utilitarianism that gives extra moral weight to reducing bads that people undergo as compared to providing them goods. For example, if several people are experiencing pain, there is more reason to help the person with the worst pain at that time, independently of how well-off or badly off that person is in terms of the lifetime well-being she is headed toward. Negatively weighted utilitarianism implies that if we had to choose between preventing well-off Felicity from breaking her leg or instead bringing it about that badly off Dolores gets a great vacation in the Alps, we should favor, to some degree, preventing Felicity from undergoing the looming bad thing. Priority firmly disagrees. Siding with priority, one could acknowledge that we humans may have psychological dispositions to respond more strongly to bads than goods, but deny this has any normative reason-giving weight.

1.4 Axiology and Morally Right Conduct

So far the discussion has been focused on a question of right conduct: Is it morally right in some circumstances to bring about a smaller benefit for a worse-off person than instead to bring about a larger benefit for an already better-off person? To this question, the proposed reply is Yes.

But a different question can also be raised, to which a version of priority might be proposed as the right answer. We can distinguish ways the world might go or states of affairs and outcomes, the latter being states of affairs that our acts or omissions might bring about. A for-sure outcome of an action is the difference your action would make to how the world goes – the difference in terms of what matters, what we should care about. These states of affairs can be assessed from many perspectives, in many different ways. A prudential ranking of states of affairs from a particular agent's perspective ranks the states of affairs as better or worse according to the degree to which she is well-off or badly off in one state of affairs compared to others. Let us consider impartial rankings. These assess states of affairs according to standards that do not rank one state of affairs above another on the basis that in one, some particular individuals or some particular group of individuals or members of some social group, identical in relevant respects to others, are better off, and in the alternate scenario, worse off. Let us further consider individualistic impartial rankings. These are impartial rankings that are determinable, given only information about individual persons (and other individual animals) and their characteristics. For simplicity, we set aside the important issues involving how to balance outcomes for human persons and outcomes for other animals.

Priority is an axiological (outcome evaluation) standard that ranks outcomes as morally better or worse according to the aggregate sum of priority-weighted well-being (welfare) they contain. The greater the aggregate sum of priority-weighted well-being, the better the outcome. This is in a way a broad-church, ecumenical view. Its doctrinal commitment is limited to the assertion that a certain curve is concave. This curved line is formed by measuring, along the horizontal axis, the well-being level of an individual, and along the vertical axis, the moral value of obtaining a further slight increment of well-being for an individual at any level of well-being.

In a way ecumenical: but embedded in priority are two controversial commitments. One is that the evaluation of the outcomes our actions might bring about depends only on their impact on the well-being of individuals. Well-being here names whatever in itself makes someone's life go better rather than worse for her. This is controversial in ruling out claimed impersonal goods as positively affecting the value of outcomes. Suppose the Grand Canyon will survive or not, depending on what you do, but its survival will never affect anyone's well-being (maybe all animal life on Earth is extinguished, and no extraterrestrials will ever land here and appreciate the Canyon's majestic beauty). A further implication is that the welfare of collectives and groups as such, over and above the welfare of the individual members of the groups, makes no difference at all to the evaluation of outcomes.

The second controversial commitment embedded in prioritarian outcome assessment is that well-being is not a moralized concept. This needs explaining. The thought is that your making choices or having attitudes that are morally right or wrong, morally creditable or discreditable, does not in itself make your own well-being increase or decrease. Your well-being depends on whether your self-interest is advanced, not your interests in being moral or giving due consideration and respect to others as morality demands. Being a moral hero does not in itself add an iota of advantage to you that registers as well-being increase, and being a moral scoundrel does not in itself subtract an iota of advantage that registers as well-being decrease. Being moral or immoral is one thing and achieving high or low well-being in your life is something else entirely.

It is plain, I hope, why this commitment seems plausible and compelling to many of us. But some find this commitment not just incorrect and implausible but preposterous. Victor Tadros (2016,1) imagines a dialogue between Genghis Khan, the great Mongol conqueror of the twelfth century, and his mother, while he is still a child. Young Genghis opines that he does not want to follow a recognized career path in his society and his mother says, "Your father and I will support you and approve of whatever you choose to do in life that makes you happy." Take "happiness" here as signifying well-being/welfare. Tadros observes that the mother's view is silly. Becoming a world conqueror by way of wrongfully slaughtering hundreds of thousands of mostly innocent persons in itself blights the life of the conqueror, in itself makes his life go horribly bad for him. Even if Genghis Khan lives a supremely happy life, or one full of satisfied desires, or one that achieves great goods of achievement, friendship, and love, being horribly immoral in itself makes your life go badly for you. On Tadros's view, well-being has to be understood as a moralized concept.

This may be one of those philosophical disputes in which adherents of opposed positions believe their opponents are not just wrong but obviously wrong. Against Tadros, I would say that avoiding a career path that includes the bloody slaughter of innocents with no remotely sufficient justification would definitely be choiceworthy but need not be prudent. It all depends. I would not urge my militarily precocious child to become a Genghis Khan for our times, but that is because my aims for my child extend beyond trying to promote her well-being and also include her becoming firmly disposed to interact with others in ways that are morally right, fair, and just.

A spare revision of priority, relaxing the first commitment, will be introduced in Section 3. This says, people's being more rather than less morally deserving enhances the impersonal moral value of welfare gains that accrue to them, just as people's being worse off enhances the impersonal moral value of such welfare gains.

Notice, the impartial standard for outcome ranking that we seek is a moral standard. We aim to find a standard that ranks outcomes of possible actions by the moral value they contain. It's morally a good thing when people fare better in welfare, and more morally valuable, according to priority, the worse off in absolute terms the beneficiaries would otherwise be.

Outcome evaluation is ranking outcomes of possible actions, and the ranking has to give rise to reasons to choose one action or another. The simplest connection between the moral ranking of outcomes and the issue of what we morally ought to choose and do is consequentialist. Consequentialism says, one morally ought always to do whatever would bring about the best reachable consequences (outcome), the one ranked highest by whatever is the correct outcome assessment standard. But there are less simple connections possible. For example, one might hold a deontological morality, according to which, one may be forbidden to do what would bring about the best reachable outcome, on the ground that doing so would violate a moral constraint we should obey, and one may not be required to bring about the best reachable outcome, because doing so would require more self-sacrifice than one is duty-bound to make.

Consider this last idea, that outcome rankings do not necessarily give rise to duties to bring about better outcomes. In this view, the outcome ranking still provides reasons for choice, just not necessarily decisive ones. Let's say the outcome ranking might at the limit just generate purely optional, take it or leave it reasons for choice, but more plausibly gives rise to a moral duty of beneficence, a duty to improve the world by bringing about impartially better rather than worse states of affairs, and the beneficence duty in turn might be deemed more or less weighty in the determination of what all things considered one morally ought to do.

To characterize the prioritarian outcome evaluation standard, it helps to contrast it with competitors (here I follow Adler 2012). First, consider utilitarianism. This standard is elegantly simple. It says, for each outcome, find the aggregate of well-being summed across persons it contains. The best outcome is the one with the highest sum, and any other outcome is worse – the greater the gap between it and the best. The associated doctrine of morally right action says: do whatever would bring about the best outcome, that is, the greatest reachable sum of well-being. Any other act is worse, the greater the gap between it and the best.

Strictly speaking, utilitarianism does not require summing across persons. All the information one needs, to determine the right course of action is what would be the impact on total welfare of each of the acts one could now choose and execute. Whether this welfare is gained by collectives or individuals, or smeared across the two types of entity, does not signify. In contrast, to apply priority one must identify individual persons and track each person across time, to know what lifetime welfare level each is heading toward. In this way priority respects the "separateness of persons." But in fact the classical utilitarians, certainly J. S. Mill (1979), did interpret utility as accruing to individuals (and other animals). The individual is the unique container of utility and in this way morally special.

Priority makes a small but significant adjustment to utilitarian outcome ranking (and to the associated doctrine of morally right action). Like utilitarianism, priority is *welfarist:* all that matters for the ranking of states of affairs is how the individual persons existing in those states of affairs are faring in terms of welfare or well-being. Consider outcomes in which the same persons exist. Pareto says that if in one state of affairs compared to a second, one person is better off in terms of welfare and no one is worse off, the first state of affairs is better than the second. Pareto indifference says that if no one is better off, and no one worse off, in terms of welfare, in one state of affairs compared to a second, the two states of affairs are equally good. Welfare anonymity says that two states of affairs are equally good if the welfare levels of persons in one is a permutation of the welfare levels of persons in the other. Welfarism consists of the three conditions just stated. Both priority and utilitarianism satisfy the Pareto norms and welfare anonymity.

Priority breaks away from utilitarianism by commitment to a broadly egalitarian norm, Pigou–Dalton. This says that a transfer of welfare without loss from a person with greater welfare to one with less, provided the transfer does not leave the person who gets the transfer at a higher welfare level than the other, and provided no one else's welfare is thereby changed, makes the resulting state of affairs an improvement. This is the condition that bends the line that graphs a person's present well-being level against the moral value of a small increase in her well-being. A continuity condition smooths this curve. This says that if one state of affairs is better than another, states of affairs close to the first are also better; the same holds if one state of affairs is worse than another. By contrast, while agreeing on continuity, the utilitarian is committed to what Krister Byqvist (2014) has called *transactional equity.* A shift in an outcome that takes well-being from one person and redistributes that same amount of well-being to others with no loss and no other well-being impact on anyone else brings about an outcome that is no worse and no better than the first. This is the case, according to transactional equity, even if the well-being is distributed from a worse-off person to a better-off person.

Utilitarian and prioritarian axiology agree in affirming *person separability*: If a shift from one state of affairs to another leaves some individuals unaffected, their welfare levels do not affect the ranking of the two states of affairs. Only the welfare of those affected in the shift makes a difference to the ranking of one state of affairs as better or worse than the other.

Here there is a contrast with egalitarian axiology (and associated doctrines of morally right action), which involves no commitment to person separability. Egalitarianism says it is in itself bad if some are worse off than others. Combined with welfarism, egalitarianism holds it is in itself bad if some are worse off in well-being than others and less inequality is better than more. (Standards for ranking states of affairs in which individuals have different amounts of welfare are various; this discussion does not explore the merits of different inequality measures.) Not being committed to separability, the egalitarian can hold that how bad it is for Tomasz to be at welfare level 1 and Ingrid at 2 and how desirable would be an outcome in which Tomasz moves to 2 and no one else is affected may vary depending on whether many others in the relevant population are sustained at 1 in both outcomes or instead there are many others in the relevant population who are sustained at 2 in both outcomes.

For the prioritarian, the relation or comparison between one person's condition and another does not in itself affect whether an outcome in which a person gains welfare is better than another in which there is no change from the status quo. In a two-person universe, a shift from Tomasz at 1 and Ingrid at 3 to another in which both are at 2 is not better on the ground that Tomasz's welfare level now compares more favorably to that of Ingrid; the betterness comes from the fact that in absolute terms, one person's moving from 1 to 2 is more valuable than that person or another's moving from 3 to 2 would be disvaluable. (This rehearses the Pigou–Dalton norm.) Increases are more valuable, the worse-off one would otherwise be.

Besides noting the similarities and differences among utilitarianism, prioritarianism, and egalitarianism, we can also contrast these views with sufficiency. Sufficientarian axiology rejects both Pigou–Dalton and transactional equity: the former, because a downward transfer of welfare from one person above sufficiency to another person who is worse off but still above sufficiency is not an improvement, and the latter, because transferring welfare from someone below sufficiency to persons above sufficiency would make the outcome worse. Sufficiency accepts person separability. But it denies continuity (which roughly holds that if one outcome is better than another, outcomes sufficiently close to the first will also be better than the other).

1.5 Priority versus Equality

Once distributive equality and priority are clearly distinguished, it becomes a subtle issue as to which view is morally superior. The egalitarian holds: (1) it is morally bad if some are worse off than others.

Claim (1) by itself does not distinguish the state of the world in which everyone is equally badly off and another state of the world in which everyone is equally well-off.[2] In both scenarios, everyone is in the same (equal) condition. But surely any sound morality should judge preferable everyone's being well-off to badly off. This point does not provide a reason to reject (1), merely a reason to supplement it. That it is morally desirable that everyone be equally well-off, and morally better that everyone is closer rather than further from being at the same benefit level, is evidently not suitable for the role of sole moral principle in a one-principle, monistic morality. Egalitarianism consorts better with a pluralist morality, combining several distinct and separate moral principles. Here the obvious candidate for inclusion is something along the line of (2) it is morally better if people are better off rather than worse off. (1) and (2) together hold that it is morally better if people are equally well-off and very well-off than if they are equally well-off and very badly off.

Let's stipulate that an individual's being better off or worse off is her having more or less well-being. Pluralist egalitarianism holds that people's having equal well-being is morally good and people's having more rather than less well-being is morally good; the two values have to be weighed and balanced against each other somehow to determine what states of the world are morally better all things considered.

Suppose in the actual current state of the world there is inequality; some individuals are better off than others. Suppose we could move away from this status quo in just one way. We could diminish a well-off person's well-being without altering anyone else's so that inequality of people's well-being levels is lessened. We could at no cost to ourselves turn off Mr. Well-off's refrigerator, so his ice cream melts, and he has less ice-cream eating enjoyment; no one else is affected at all. Call this a case of leveling down – inequality is decreased by lessening the well-being of someone whose well-being level is above average (while he still remains above average), without anyone's well-being increasing. The leveling down objection against equality asserts that someone's becoming worse off without anyone else's becoming better off cannot be in any respect bringing about a morally better state of affairs. There is just nothing positively desirable about leveling down.

---

[2] In Douglas Rae's words, "equality is indifferent between vineyards and graveyards" (Rae et alia 1981).

The egalitarian can respond that all things considered, instances of leveling down are never shifts to a better state of affairs, but it should be acknowledged that in one respect, the situation has improved. Inequality is lessened. All things considered, the situation has not improved, because the loss of Mr. Well-off's well-being outweighs the slight gain thereby attained in overall equality of well-being across persons. Moreover, we can be confident that we never will be forced by our pluralist egalitarianism to judge that a leveling down that brings about a large decrease in inequality could ever be morally desirable all things considered. As inequality declines, the well-being losses that bring this about will increase, so there will be some plausible weighting of the values in play that guarantees that leveling down can never be morally desirable all things considered. The egalitarian response charges the critic with failing to attend to the distinction between a change being desirable in one or another respect and a change being desirable all things considered. Once one attends properly to this distinction, one can see that there is nothing counterintuitive in claiming that in one respect a leveling down change is an improvement. It improves the state of the world according to the equality standard, so trivially has to be an improvement in one respect.

Some suppose that the leveling down objection rests on the background claim that one state of the world cannot be better than another in any respect if no individual is better off in the one state than the other, and this background claim is implausible taken on its own, so the leveling down objection hangs unsupported (Temkin 1993, ch. 9). For example, one might be a retributivist about punishment, holding that it is in itself an improvement on the status quo if a change brings it about that a culpable offender is punished, made to suffer, for his offense after being found guilty by a fair procedure. That is, the offender's becoming worse off in this way can in itself constitute an improvement on the prior state of affairs.

However, this line of thought may involve a misinterpretation of the leveling down objection (Parfit 2012, and for a contrary view, Hirose 2015). The prioritarian can hold that thinking about leveling down cases and rejecting equality in response to them does not assume any general background claim as the previous paragraph assumes. The prioritarian can hold that the leveling down objection is driven by a local, particular value judgment about equality, so no general claim (to the effect that no state of affairs can be better than another unless some individual is better off in the one state than in the other) needs to be assumed by the prioritarian critic.

The prioritarian can appeal to the thought that one might be attracted to the ideal of distributive equality without recognizing that equality can be increased without making any worse-off person better off. This erstwhile adherent of equality might have in her mind examples in which some better-off people lose well-being and as a result some worse-off people gain, the overall situation then becoming more equal in well-being. In these cases the losses of the better off intuitively are not good in themselves, but bads that are outweighed by gains to worse offs. (And this judgment depends on the numbers: huge losses in well-being suffered by better offs accompanied by trivial gains accruing to worse offs are not plausibly regarded as an improvement.) For this naïve, unreflective adherent of equality, just noticing that the claimed equality value can increase simply by a reduction in some people's well-being forces a reconsideration of her commitment. The naïve egalitarian we are imagining no longer espouses equality once the leveling down implication of equality views is noted. This "egalitarian" explains, "I realize now that all along what really mattered morally in my view was the moral urgency of bringing about gains for worse-off people. Equality gains brought about by no well-being gains for worse offs are no gains at all, I realize."

Another objection to egalitarianism reinforces this response and clarifies the character of the grounds for rejecting distributive equality (Parfit 1995). Suppose one asks: Is there some scope limitation on the application of a distributive equality principle? Answering this question exposes implausible features of any distributive equality view. On the one hand, any scope limitation on the jurisdiction of equality seems morally arbitrary. If equality among Hungarians is desirable, why not equality among Europeans, and equality among all inhabitants of the Earth, and for that matter across all persons no matter where in the universe they are located? If some being worse off than others matters morally in itself, then it would seem arbitrary and unmotivated to deny that it matters anywhere and everywhere. Scope restrictions in time also seem to fall by the wayside. If inequality among people now matters, why not among those living at any time this month, or this year, or at any time?[3]

On the other hand, inequality aversion with unrestricted scope seems silly. Is it bad that ancient Egyptians are worse off than present-day inhabitants of the Earth? But if one accepts distributive equality with restricted scope, say among members of a political society at a time, the suspicion arises that one's intuitive judgments in favor of equality are illicitly tracking judgments about other morally important matters that may likely be causally connected to changes in distributive equality in a limited setting. If people are interacting together and involved in the common project of sustaining a functioning political society, the degree of inequality in distribution among them may have complicated

---

[3] This is not a rhetorical question. Some say egalitarian distribution concerns only arise among people "who stand in some essentially practice-mediated relation" (Risse 2012, 7) and some hold these concerns are only binding among people who share membership in a single state.

instrumental connections, negative and positive, to the success of the project. Inequality may diminish solidarity, cooperation, dispositions of reciprocity, and other valuable social features. Equality may block incentives to behave in ways that are useful to others.

Inequality aversion with unrestricted scope implies that the strength of the moral reasons to boost someone's welfare, here and now, may depend on how well-off or badly off are distant peoples whose condition could not be affected by anything we might do. If that result strikes the reader as counterintuitive, my surmise is that the reader is registering agreement with placing a separability of person's condition on outcome assessment.

Just as the leveling down objection is not a general objection against ever leveling down (making some worse off and no one better off) for any reason, the scope objection is not a general objection against wide scope (for a contrary view, again see Hirose 2015). The leveling down objection arises from a particular concern that equalizing people's condition does not on reflection strike us as a good reason at all to make some worse off and no one better off. The scope concern arises from contemplating equalizing people's condition when people are not interacting in a community or locality.

Contemplating inequality in how well-off people are who are separated by great distances in space and time and untrammeled even by thin social connections suggests the thought that from the moral perspective, it does not in itself (intrinsically) matter how one's condition compares to that of others. And if how one's condition compares to that of others does not in itself matter, then a fortiori whether one's condition compares to that of others specifically by being equal or unequal to theirs does not matter either. This is the idea of separability: The moral value of (a change in) a person's well-being does not in itself depend on how anyone else is doing in well-being terms.

In a more complete discussion, other possibilities would merit investigation. One possible view is that equality matters for its own sake in certain contexts and not others. Equality has this moral value only when certain conditions hold. In some contexts, equality is unfair, while in others, not. Or one might hold that in certain contexts equality aligns with solidarity and then has value, as when one wants to be in the same boat with one's mates and not escape from peril alone. The version of solidarity alluded to here sounds perverse to me, and the appeal to fairness would be weightless unless one could explain what exactly renders equality fair in some situations and neither fair nor unfair in others. But further discussion is needed before declaring even a provisionally definitive verdict.

2 Some Clarifications and Further Questions

So far, priority has been characterized somewhat vaguely. Many questions arise, regarding how to interpret the priority view. This section surveys and explores a few of these questions.

2.1 Priority for What Beings?

The priority view is egalitarian in holding that in the determination of morally right actions and just and fair public policies, the interests of all comparably situated persons, within the scope of the policy choice at issue, count exactly the same. The view treats persons as special, and in some way having equal status.

So the question forces itself on our attention, what makes a thing a person entitled to this equal consideration? What makes humans morally special? One plausible answer is that most humans are persons, beings with developed rational agency capacities at or above a threshold level (Nozick 1974, 48–49; Rawls 1999, 441–449). Rational agency capacities (RAC) include cognitive, affective, and volitional elements. A rational agent has some ability to perceive features of the world and to make normative judgments and to reason about what to do in her circumstances. A rational agent has some ability to empathize with the situation of other sentient and rational creatures and sympathize with their plight. A rational agent also has volitional capacity. She has the ability to make up her mind as to what she will do and will to execute this plan and the ability to act on her resolve and persist in carrying out what she has decided to do despite difficulty and discomfort.

For personhood status, having some mix of RAC that passes a threshold suffices. At least within a broad range, possessing above-threshold capacities does not entitle a being to any higher status; all within the range have the same basic entitlements. Personhood so understood is a status that most human individuals gradually acquire when young and retain unless and until severe RAC impairment lowers them below the threshold, rendering them former persons.

Giving special status to beings that qualify as persons in this way is controversial. An alternative view is that any being that is capable of gaining a good that improves its welfare is thereby morally considerable. Obtaining identical amounts of good (avoiding identical amounts of bad) for any morally considerable being is equally morally valuable and counts the same in the determination of the overall moral value of outcomes of choices that agents could make. Peter Singer has expressed this thought with the slogan, "All animals are equal." The RAC view will hold instead that the welfare goods of beings that qualify as persons count for more than identical welfare goods that might be gained by morally considerable beings that are nonpersons.

"All animals are equal" combined with priority has radical implications. Surely nonhuman animals as we know them are morally considerable, count for something. But if achieving gains for those individuals who are badly off in welfare is morally more important, as priority says, and if on any noncrazy view animals uniformly have low welfare compared to humans, priority will recommend giving priority to achieving gains for (for example) ordinary mice over ordinary humans (Vallentyne 2005). If priority is to be interpreted sympathetically, we should probably accept the Rawls-Nozick view as to what makes it the case that a being's being badly off generates special moral reason to improve its condition. However, this view implies that relieving pains of very severely cognitively impaired humans has lesser priority than relieving pains of persons, and this implication is controversial.

2.2 Scope of Concern

Which persons' well-being gains and losses matter for determining what is morally right to do? In principle, priority could be applied country by country, clan by clan, race by race, family by family. In cases where extraterrestrials confront Earthlings, priority could be applied to Earthlings (human individuals as we know them), giving no weight to interests of extraterrestrials. But as a moral doctrine, the natural scope for priority is universal. Benefits and losses falling on any person count, and if the persons share morally relevant attributes, count the same in the determination of what one owes to them and how they ought to be treated. This allows, local concern may be justified on instrumental grounds.

A wide-scope cosmopolitan morality treats time the same way. In principle, if one could bring about an equally morally weighted benefit for a person now or instead one living 100 or 10,000 years from now, and all else is equal, the benefit for the person living now and the person living much later count the same in fixing the moral value of outcomes of actions one might choose.

If the reader is uneasy about universal scope, note that outcome rankings of morally best outcomes might be combined with principles for selecting actions as morally mandatory, prohibited, or optional, that allow partiality to self and others. The universal scope being suggested as appropriate is universal scope at the level of outcome rankings. This leaves it a completely open question, whether the outcome ranking completely determines what one morally ought to do, or gives rise to a significant duty of impartial beneficence, or a weak duty, or a moral reason of barely discernible tiny strength. Act consequentialism combined with cosmopolitan outcome evaluation does yield an austere and demanding doctrine of moral rightness. (That a doctrine is austere and demanding is not per se a criticism of it.)

2.3 Better Off and Worse Off: Priority of What?

People's condition might be assessed in many ways. People can vary in their bank account wealth, their resource holdings, their overall opportunities, their basic need fulfillment by one or another standard of basic need, their freedom by various measures of freedom, or the degree to which their moral rights are fulfilled, to give some examples. A prioritarian axiology or an account of right conduct could be developed using any of these measures. So far I have taken for granted that the measure to employ is people's welfare or well-being (what one seeks insofar as one is striving to be prudent). What might justify this choice?

This is a large question. We are pondering what standard to employ to evaluate people's condition as outcomes of actions people might do, with a view to determining what we morally ought to do. The question is, what do we owe one another?

The choice of individual welfare or well-being as the proper outcome measure reflects a claim that freedoms, opportunities, resources, and the like, when not components of well-being or partly constitutive of components, are to be assessed as only hindrances or helps for gaining what really matters. "Welfare/well-being" just names whatever this is. It's what should ultimately matter to anyone, so far as she is aiming at her own self-interest, trying to be prudent, making her life go better rather than worse for her. In different circumstances, things that are often helps to well-being increases become hindrances. (With a small professor's income, Arneson drinks beer and lives pretty well, but given his proclivities, with a large movie star's income he would overuse heroin and cocaine and live badly.) This holds also for moral rights fulfillment. In some circumstances, violating my rights might result in a better outcome for me, on any conception of moral rights. We need to say more here, even if the discussion must be quick and inadequate.

Rather than take well-being as the outcome measure, we could instead hold that our fundamental duty to others is to facilitate their satisfying their actual aims and preferences. This expresses proper respect for persons. So some hold. The objection to this gambit is that people's actual aims and preferences are sometimes directed at worthless or immoral objects. Respecting my status as a partially rational agent requires steering me away from such irrational ventures not helping me down wrong paths. A revised version of the proposal would be that our fundamental duty to others is to facilitate their fulfilling whatever it is they most care about, whether or not this has anything to do with their own welfare, so long as their fundamental cares and concerns are reasonable. The trouble with the revised proposal is that if we suppose people reasonably may care to varying degrees about helping others or helping themselves, evenhandedly trying to help all achieve what they care about ends up promoting unfairness (Dworkin 2000, 21–25). Some seek to achieve social justice worldwide at great personal cost to themselves, while Dick seeks his own advantage to the maximum that is morally permissible. The revised proposal requires us, in welfare terms, to boost Dick's advantage level at unfair expense to others.

Another proposal along this line holds that what we owe to others is assisting their getting a fair share of resources and opportunities, and leaving it to each person to use her fair share as she pleases. This proposal inherits some of what was implausible in the revised proposal. Another objection is that we are here making a fetish of what does not ultimately matter. Suppose it is suggested that what we owe others is the formal freedom to act as they choose without interference. The objection is that what matters surely is not formal freedom but rather what people are actually enabled to be and do in their circumstances. The amended thought now is that the measure of people's condition for determining who is badly off, who well-off, and to what degree, is the extent of their real or effective freedom to achieve what they have reason to value. But the fetishism objection recurs. Having the most marvelous abundant real freedom, such that for a huge range of valuable goals, if I choose the goal and pursue it by some plan I can adopt and follow, I achieve it, I might be disposed not to make good use of this real freedom, or have difficulty choosing well, or following through, and so my actual life comes to grief. For me, better less real freedom and greater well-being. We have circled around back to the idea of well-being as the proper outcome measure. In a slogan, morality, or at least the impartial beneficence component of morality, requires us to seek genuinely good lives for people, with good (well-being) fairly distributed. This is clearly a big, complex, controversial topic, about which more needs to be said. The discussion here must make do with flagging the issue and moving on.

So let's assume the outcome measure should fix on individual well-being. To apply priority, we need to be able to make cardinal interpersonal comparisons of individual well-being. We must be able to determine, at least in principle, not only that Sally is made better off than Sam in some outcome, but by how much (unit comparability). To decide how great a moral reason there is for bringing about a gain in well-being of a given size for a person, we must be able, at least in principle, to determine the level of well-being the person would otherwise reach, absent this benefit (level comparability). Perhaps the requirement of cardinal interpersonal comparability is too demanding. Perhaps there are outcomes that are incomparable in well-being for the people they contain. Even if so, considering what outcome assessment standards would be correct on the assumption of full comparability might help us to begin to determine what outcome assessment standards would be correct, dropping that assumption. Some cardinal interpersonal well-being comparisons must be possible or else the issue on which priority takes a stand cannot even be posed.

2.4 Well-Being, What?

Priority says that a well-being gain for a person is morally more valuable, the lower the well-being level she would otherwise reach. Well-being, or alternatively "welfare," is the idea of whatever in itself makes a person's life go better for her rather than worse. It's what one seeks when one is trying to be prudent.

There are different theories as to what constitutes well-being. One is hedonism (the good for a person is feeling good – pleasure and absence of pain). Another is preference satisfaction or life aim fulfillment – getting whatever one wants for oneself for its own sake. Another family of views is pluralistic and objective. According to these views, there are several things, such as friendship, love, achievement, significant knowledge, and pleasure, and the more one obtains these goods, weighted by their comparative value, the better one's life goes for one.

The discussions in the section to come leave the idea of well-being as a blank to be filled in as the reader chooses. This is an important topic, for public policy and to some extent, surely, for decisions about how to live one's life. It's not a topic this Element addresses.

The outcome assessment views surveyed in this Element all take the well-being of individual persons to be the entirety of what in itself contributes to the moral goodness of outcomes or the largest part of that. To give this background view a fair hearing, don't make the mistake of embracing a silly or implausible conception of welfare and then dismiss the claim that welfare has the centrality for ethics that prioritarians and utilitarians suppose it does. Think instead in terms of the most plausible and compelling view of well-being you can identify. Of course, doing this does not guarantee you will find welfarism plausible.

2.5 Temporal Unit

Suppose it is accepted that priority should be applied evenhandedly across all persons, or perhaps all human persons. Suppose we have a uniquely compelling conception of what constitutes the well-being of a person – what in itself makes her life go better rather than worse for her. Suppose we have a standard for measuring well-being on this conception, so in principle we can discover the number that corresponds to your well-being at a time. Summing these numbers over time yields your well-being. Sum over what time period? Priority could take different forms depending on the time frame adopted. Priority could apply to individual lifetimes, or stages of lives, such as childhood, prime age adulthood, and old age, or to individuals at a time, or to individuals at moments of time, or some combination of these alternatives.

The case for adopting a lifetime perspective is that it is natural to view a person's life as extending over time. If we plot the successive times of an individual's life on the Y axis and how well-off that person is at each moment of time on the X axis, we get a line extending from the individual's birth to death, and the overall well-being of the person is just the area under the curve. Low welfare at some times can on this view be offset by higher welfare at other times, and the reverse can happen as well.

One view of rational prudence requires temporal neutrality: one should regard each time of one's life as equally important for one's overall welfare as any other time, and seek to maximize the sum of welfare across all the times of one's life. Insofar as one has control over how long one lives, one should strive to exercise that control to facilitate maximizing the lifetime total of welfare. Perhaps some components of individual welfare cannot be precisely located. If writing a good novel increases one's welfare, exactly when does the welfare gain accrue to one? But the view can be adjusted to take account of this. Think of the equal-sized times of one's life as so many containers, and one seeks to maximize the sum of personal good or welfare in the containers; if some goods are ambiguously smeared across several containers, that does not make it impossible to add up the welfare gains and losses in all the containers.

Objection: On the view being proposed, for any very long life with a constant high level of well-being that Sally might lead, it would be better for her instead to have a much longer life, maybe tens of thousands of years in length or longer, with each year of her life just barely worth living. (If she had one potato less, her life for that year would be worse for her than having no life at all.) The total of well-being Sally gets in the second life would be greater. But this implication discredits the view that generates it.

Reply: You could avoid this implication by requiring that for any year (or pick some other time period) of a person's life to be good for her to have, it must exceed some threshold level of positive well-being. Or you might hold that there are some special goods, and unless your life gains enough of the special goods, it cannot be a good life, one worth living, no matter what quantity of the nonspecial goods one gets instead. Other fixes are possible. I suggest that when you examine each proposed fix, it will have some implications more counterintuitive than the simple view being proposed. Better to stay simple.

A familiar feature of ordinary life is that one trades off goods and bads at different times of one's life with a view to maximizing the total. A sacrifice of years of onerous education may be redeemed by the gains in income and welfare benefits that income can bring to one. Years of rewarding physical activity or pleasant inebriation can be part of an overall maximization of lifetime welfare even if they bring about some period of physical deterioration in later years.

The lifetime view as described takes it for granted that the relation of personal identity holds across all the times of one's life, or perhaps, over all the bits of one's life united by spatio-temporal continuity of a functioning brain. The view also assumes that rational prudence follows personal identity. All times of my life in this sense are equally times of me. One alternative view takes a psychological view of identity, such that a life broken by great psychological disconnection, though all stages in the history of a single functioning brain, would not in the relevant sense be all stages of me. Yet another view is that the degree to which it is rational for a person to have prudential concern for future stages of his life varies with the degree to which there is psychological continuity across the stages. On this account, psychologically distant states of myself are all stages of me, but not in a way that rationalizes my having special concern for them.

One might apply priority not to lifetimes, or not only to lifetimes, but to stages of people's lives, such as childhood, prime adulthood, and old age. Or one might apply priority at moments of time. On this latter view, if somebody is badly off now, there is special reason to help that person now, independently of how things have been going for the person at other times of her life.

Dennis McKerlie asks us to imagine a large gap between the well-being levels of middle-aged people and old people living simultaneously. We can suppose that although the former are enjoying a far higher quality of life than the latter, this good life had been enjoyed by the old when they were younger, so that both age cohorts are on the way to living lives that will be the same in lifetime totals of well-being. So from the complete lives perspective, there is no inequality here to which principles of justice should be sensitive. For simplicity, assume that all of the middle-aged people are at the same current and cumulative well-being level and all of the old people are at a lower current well-being level, the same for each one. McKerlie continues, "To make the case vivid, imagine that the same city block contains a condominium complex and a retirement home. The residents of the complex are middle-aged, middle class, affluent, and happy. The retirement home is old and overcrowded, and badly managed. Its residents receive adequate medical care, but their situation offers them little dignity and little opportunity for anything approaching happiness" (McKerlie

2013, 6–7). The suggestion is that evaluating people's condition only by their lifetime totals renders one tone-deaf to distributive injustice, whether assessed by egalitarian or prioritarian principles.

It is not so clear that this example puts pressure on a lifetime perspective advocate to abandon her stance. As described, the example suggests that although all are heading to equally good lives over their lifetimes, people's lifetime well-being would be increased if resources were transferred from middle-aged to old. The condo dwellers seem to have more money than they need, and the elderly are suffering in ways a little bit of extra cash could alleviate. If we clarify the example to remove this feature, the intuition that justice requires transfer from the middle-aged to the elderly now, on the ground that at the present time, the elderly are worse off, no longer looks plausible. Suppose the elderly in the nursing home all suffer from debilitating arthritis, for which all available remedies are very costly and not very effective. (Pain relief medication decreases mental alertness and has other hard to treat side effects, surgical procedures have very low success rate, and so on.) Any attempt to equalize the well-being of condo dwellers and nursing home residents now would unavoidably make everyone worse off not better off in lifetime terms. Then from the lifetime perspective, the elderly are compensated for their present aches and pains by the greater well-being they had when younger.

Setting the example to the side, I just reiterate that depending on what we take the appropriate temporal unit to be, prioritarian outcome evaluation will yield different judgments, and these will lead to different judgments about what should be done, insofar as we have moral reasons to bring about better rather than worse outcomes. Priority could be given to those whose overall lifetimes are turning out especially bad, or to those especially badly off at different life stages, or to those badly off at any given moment of time, or to some combination of these. Moreover, the same options will arise in developing an egalitarian view or a sufficiency doctrine.

Lifetime priority requires reckoning at a discount the value of further gains for the elderly who have already amassed high cumulative well-being. This stance will justify what in ordinary terms might seem discrimination against the old. If one possible outcome of choice is preserving the endangered lives of the old people in the nursing home McKerlie imagines for one month, and another possible outcome is preserving the endangered lives of children in an orphanage for one month, with the amount of well-being gained the same whichever outcome occurs, lifetime priority counts the gain to the children as morally more valuable, if they are heading to lifetime well-being less than the old people will be attaining.

2.6 Population and Population Ethics

Throughout most of the discussions in this Element, the assumption is made that in comparing and assessing outcomes, we face situations in which the exact same people exist in all the outcomes being compared (counting dead people, who have existed, as existing). The appeal of priority for those to whom it appears attractive, and the objections launched by critics, are manifest in these situations. But this leaves a substantial gap. Many policies affect the numbers and the identity of future people. A simple decision that results in childbirth perhaps affects the numbers of people and virtually always affects identity. (If a couple delays childbearing until they finish school, the child born earlier would originate in a different sperm–and–egg combination from the child that would have come about from later conception.)

Population ethics is notoriously difficult. But it would be premature to embrace priority on the basis of its adequacy in yielding verdicts about outcome assessment (and beyond that, verdicts about what is morally right to do or inputs into such verdicts) when the same people exist in all of the outcomes being compared. If priority is acceptable, it has to be acceptable in all the significant contexts in which it might be applied (for a contrary view, see Parfit 2012).

Many people believe that there are strong moral reasons to help people who exist now or who definitely will exist in future to have good lives, but that there is no moral reason to bring into existence a new person who will have a life worth living, one with positive well-being. In the words of Jan Narveson, it is morally imperative to make people happy, but not to make happy people. But this is hard to swallow; surely bringing into existence a person who will have a life well worth living, even at some cost to definitely existing persons, is improving the world from the moral standpoint. As the Judeo-Christian Bible tells us, "Be fruitful, and multiply" (Genesis 1:28*)*.

Priority says, if bringing a person into existence with positive well-being X is the equivalent of moving an existing person from zero well-being to X, then the former, all else equal, is morally superior to improving by that same number of well-being units an existing person who already has positive well-being. Priority adds, there is an asymmetry between bringing into existence a person who will have positive well-being (say +10) and a person who will have negative well-being (say -10), the former is less morally valuable than the latter is morally disvaluable (Holtug 2007). Priority, no doubt, has some counterintuitive implications when extended to variable-population scenarios, but if "ordinary common sense" on these issues is latently inconsistent, prioritarian population ethics may be acceptable all things considered, compared to alternatives. Notwithstanding its interest and importance, the topic of priority and population ethics is not explored in the present work.

2.7 The Weighting Issue: How Much Priority?

Priority says a well-being gain that might be obtained for a person is morally more valuable the larger the gain, and more valuable the worse in absolute terms the person's lifetime well-being level would otherwise be. This is a broad-church, ecumenical doctrine. Its main commitment is that the line that tracks increases in well-being for a person on the horizontal axis and the moral value of increases on the vertical axis is concave – slopes upward and bends down. This commits us to very little as to the degree to which gains in well-being from increasing well-being baselines have marginally decreasing moral value. But it clearly matters enormously how much priority goes to increasing well-being as compared to assigning extra value to a gain of a given size, the worse off in absolute terms the recipient.

A priority view with slight priority to the worse off differs very little from utilitarian ranking. A priority with great priority for the worse-off approaches a leximin view. (Leximin is an extreme version of Pareto-respecting egalitarianism. It says, as a first priority, make the worst off as well-off as possible; having maximized for the worst off, as a second priority, make the second-worst-off individual as well-off as possible; and so on, until as a lowest priority, maximize the condition of the best off. "Worst-off" refers not to the individual who now happens to be most disadvantaged but to whoever fills the slot of being worst off as time passes.)

Notice that Pigou–Dalton, the condition that separates the family of priority views from the utilitarian assessment standard, is strictly a very mild condition. It says a transfer of well-being from one individual who is better off than another to one who is worse off, without any loss of well-being, and without reversing their positions, and without affecting anyone else, is an improvement. When I introduced the priority idea in Section 1, with the story of Dolores and Felicity, I appealed to the reader to support the intuition that it would be morally valuable to help Dolores, given how grim her life has been, at Felicity's expense, given how well his life has been, even if the transfer would considerably lessen his well-being and only slightly boost hers. But the basis of this appeal is not captured just by Pigou–Dalton – rather by Pigou–Dalton plus a vague claim that "significantly" greater loss by better offs to gain improvement for worse offs is justified. If some are in heaven and some are in hellish conditions through no fault of choice of their own, it would be morally desirable to bring the sufferers out of their hellish condition even if their gain is considerably less than what the heaven dwellers have to put up with by way of diminution of bliss.

Specifying the morally right trade-off ration here – what ratio of loss falling on top dogs to benefits accruing to underdogs would make the overall outcome better – is an issue that is politically as well as morally divisive. Of course, the issue gets overshadowed by claims of entitlement; well-off Dick says, I have a right to what's mine, and no one is morally permitted to take from me or do what harms me in rights-violating ways no matter what are the unmet needs of however many are in a condition similar to that of Dolores. But if we think these claims of entitlement ultimately boil down to social convention, we are back to the trade-off ratio issue.

As often in moral and political philosophy, we end up in a position where, plural values having been identified, even if we are sure the identified values are the only ones that matter, we still are very far from having a determinate view of being able to generate determinate outcome rankings or, with further assumptions, judgments about what is morally required, forbidden, and optional to do.

3 Priority for the Deserving

3.1 Incorporating Deservingness into Prioritarianism

Our initial discussion of what is wrong with utilitarianism pointed to two problems, both arising from this doctrine's commitment to maximization of well-being across persons regardless of how that well-being is distributed. One problem was that utilitarianism gives no special weight to bringing about gains (and avoiding losses) for people who are very badly off in absolute terms (or maybe badly off compared to others). Another problem was that utilitarianism gives no special weight to bringing about gains for people who are specially deserving. For the utilitarian, utility gains for scoundrels are counted exactly the same as gains for saints in the determination of morally required policies and actions (compare Ross 1930). We have considered priority for badly off people. What about the second problem?

An obvious response to this second problem is to incorporate priority for the morally deserving along with priority for the badly off into the priority view. In parallel with the idea of priority for being badly off, the idea of priority for deservingness need not be an inherently comparative notion. Deservingness affects the moral value of such welfare gains and losses as accrue to one over the course of one's life. Suppose there is a standard of deservingness, and that the degree to which one satisfies this standard gives one a deservingness score, perhaps altering over the course of one's life, measured by a number that is cardinally interpersonally comparable. Deservingness scores might be taken to range only above zero, reflecting the fact that just qualifying as a person confers on one some pro tanto entitlement to well-being, and that a person's gaining an increment of well-being never has negative moral value. Deservingness priority says that the moral value of any well-being gain that accrues to a person is greater, the higher her deservingness score – and correspondingly, the disvalue of well-being losses that accrue to a person are greater – the higher her deservingness score.

This yields a double prioritarianism. The moral value of a well-being gain that accrues to a person is larger, the larger the well-being gain, and larger, the worse off the person otherwise would be in lifetime well-being, and larger, the higher the person's overall deservingness. Benefits matter more, the worse off the person to whom they accrue, and the more deserving that person is.

Priority for the deserving is first of all an axiological view. The question is, how to assess the intrinsic moral value of states of affairs or outcomes (outcomes are states of affairs resulting from a causal process that is of interest). Priority for a person, the more badly off she is, is one of a family of welfarist standards of assessment. Weak welfarism holds that the moral value of a state of affairs is some increasing function of the welfare or well-being of the individual persons in that state of affairs.

Here I mention that the invocation of priority for the deserving immediately puts pressure on the commitment to weak welfarism (Arneson 2007, 2019) and in my view justifies its abandonment. The denial of weak welfarism holds that something entirely separate and independent from the well-being of individual persons affects the moral value of state of affairs, The difficulties encountered when one attempts to incorporate priority for the deserving into a welfarist axiology point toward reasons to maintain that independently of the amount and distribution of individual well-being in a state of affairs. The degree to which people are more or less deserving in itself affects the moral value inhering in a state of affairs. All else equal, it's a better world, in itself, when people are more rather than less deserving, nicer rather than nastier.

As already mentioned, the axiological ranking of outcomes as better or worse so far says nothing about what one morally ought to do or what policies we should implement. The simplest view here is act consequentialist: One morally ought always to do whatever would bring about the best reachable outcome. A deontological moral doctrine affirms that we have moral duties beyond duties to improve the world, bring about better outcomes. Instead moral requirements consist of rules forbidding acts, such as promise-breaking, deemed wrong in themselves apart from consequences. If a nonconsequentialist moral doctrine includes a duty of beneficence, keyed to bringing about better rather than worse outcomes, the axiology plays some role in determining what is right, greater or smaller depending on the weight ascribed to beneficence versus other deonto-logical rules. One might hold that the connection between outcome axiology and the existence of *some* duty of beneficence is hard to deny.

The axiological ranking of outcomes, it should be noted, is a ranking of states of affairs for the purposes of guiding judgment about morally right actions and policies. Though not in itself a ranking of actions as more or less choiceworthy, it is in its conception an input into rankings of actions as more or less right and wrong or as more or less morally choiceworthy. If there are values that rightly play no role in the determination of moral rankings of actions, such values do not affect the rankings of outcomes. Outcomes are partially characterized states of affairs that might be brought about by actions under review.

To explore the thought that it is in itself morally more valuable, all else equal, for a deserving person to get a welfare boost than for a less deserving person to get one, care must be taken to set aside instrumental considerations. Many people's ideas of deservingness are such that one's deserving conduct tends to make other people better off. But the issue is, is it intrinsically morally more valuable for a saint rather than a sinner to get a needed life preserver even if both are equally well-off, both would get the same welfare boost from getting the aid, and there are no further consequences to consider?

If both priority to the badly off and to the more deserving have weight in determining right actions, what is the comparative weight of each priority type? A full theory needs to specify the weights.

3.2 Priority for the Deserving under Attack

Prioritarianism incorporating desert as just characterized will in some circum-stances recommend actions that increase someone's deservingness without making anyone better off and even at a cost of making some, or even everyone, worse off. This just follows from the fact that there are plural factors that matter and they trade-off against each other – none takes absolute priority over the others. (The trade-off could go the other way. If the numbers are right, double priority could require actions that bring about a world in which all of us are jerks and scoundrels, and far less deserving that we might have been, provided the well-being gains for people, adjusted to reflect priority for the worse off, are sufficiently large.)

This expansive prioritarianism conflicts with the Pareto norm. For some, that is the end of the story. Matthew Adler, himself a prominent theorist and proponent of prioritarianism, is blunt: "Desert-modulated prioritarianism is a nonstarter" (Adler 2018).

Adler notes two core requirements of a prioritarian ranking that conflict with catering to desert. Well-being Pareto Indifference says, If each person is equally well-off in outcome x as she is in outcome y, then x and y are equally good. Well-being Strong Pareto says, if each person is at least as well-off in y as she is in x, and at least one person is strictly better off in y, then y is better than x.

According to Adler, axiological priority is an outcome ranking doctrine (Adler 2012; Adler and Holtug 2019). The moral value of any outcome (for fixed population) depends entirely on the welfare of each person who exists in that outcome. This welfarist requirement is specified by Pareto Indifference and Strong Pareto. The moral core of the doctrine is that it ranks the moral value of outcomes in this welfarist way and also respects two further requirements. One is Pigou–Dalton, the other is person separability. These two conditions can be reformulated so as to be compatible with priority for the deserving. But the thought that the world might be improved, made morally better all things considered, by lowering some people's welfare without bringing about welfare gains for anyone, is anathema for a Paretian ethic.

3.2.1 Response to Adler

The sheer fact of conflict is not an objection, so far as I can see, to a view that says both priority for the worse off and priority for the more deserving are factors that in themselves affect the value of outcomes and hence what we ought to do all things considered. This is a simple consequence of the position that the two factors matter intrinsically and independently and that they trade-off against each other; neither has lexical priority over the other. And exactly the same goes for the claim that well-being increases (and preventions of losses) matter morally in themselves and matter according to the adjustment dictated by priority for the worse off. Well-being increases are intrinsically morally desirable, but not the only moral desideratum: priority for the deserving over the undeserving also matters in the same way, in itself and independently of any other factors that might be relevant to outcome assessment.

But if one has a strong conviction that the Pareto norm is correct, then pointing out that giving weight to deservingness conflicts with it will register as a decisive objection against desert-modulated prioritarianism (but see Temkin 2001).

If you think the leveling down objection is the main ground for affirming priority, by way of rejecting its egalitarian rivals, you may well be resistant to accepting priority for the deserving. But as noted in Section 1, that would anyway be a misguided way to view the dialectical situation. Noticing that the egalitarian finds something to value in a move that makes better-off people worse off and does nothing to improve the welfare of the worse off, namely that we are getting close to equal distribution, simply makes us realize that we don't value in itself how people's situation compares to that of others, so a fortiori we do not and should not value in itself people's being equally well-off or getting closer to that condition. This judgment does not commit us to Pareto. That someone's welfare goes up and nobody else's goes down is a pro tanto good, but it might be outweighed by countervailing considerations. Desert turns out to be the countervailing consideration.

3.2.2 Ideas of Deservingness

Notions of deservingness are various (Feldman 1995, 2016; Moriarty 2018). The runner in a race who crosses the finish line first, without cheating, deserves the first-place award. We tend to hold that the most qualified applicant should be offered the job. In a criminal justice system, convicted offenders who are actually guilty as charged and appropriately sentenced deserve their assigned punishment. Perhaps every human person, just by being a person, deserves good fortune.

3.2.3 Is Rewarding the Deserving Intrinsically Morally Valuable?

In many areas of enterprise, there are standards of deservingness. The standards are geared to advancing the aims of the enterprise. For example, if you want to establish a sport and encourage excellent performance in the sport, you had better set up the rules so that those more proficient win accolades. The deserving are those who work hard at the sport and perform better at it. Rewarding the deserving is a procedure that is a means to bringing it about that the sport is played and played well. If this holds across the board, then deservingness does not have a place in the formulation of fundamental moral principles. Deservingness has just instrumental value when it is valuable at all.

There is another reason to doubt that ideas about what someone deserves have a place in a fundamental moral principle that ranks possible outcomes of actions and policies as an input into the determination of morally right actions and policies. Much of what we are ordinarily said to deserve is fixed by prevailing social norms and institutional rules in our society, but these norms and institutions themselves are often morally defective. One possibility is that what we truly deserve is to be treated according to morally right norms and institutions, where what makes norms and institutions morally right has nothing to do with desert (Rawls 1999, and for an opposed view, Kagan 2012)). On this way of thinking, desert plays no fundamental role in determining how we ought to be treated and how we ought to treat one another.

We are looking for a standard of deservingness that is more than instrumentally valuable and that stands independent of existing customs and practices and provides reason to shape them in a particular direction. Here's a start: the deservingness that plausibly makes it intrinsically extra fitting that a deserving person fares well in life, attains more rather than less well-being, is only *moral* deservingness. When people are morally virtuous or in some other way morally praiseworthy, they thereby bring it about that it is especially morally urgent that their lives go better for them rather than worse. The discussion earlier already anticipated this point, by identifying the deserving as saints and the undeserving as scoundrels.

3.2.4 Objection: The Proposal That Getting Benefits for the Morally Deserving Has Special Moral Urgency Runs Afoul of the Control Principle (No Moral Luck)

Whether you are morally virtuous and more so than others are, standardly depends on factors beyond people's power to control. Being smarter, some can figure out, for example, what courage requires, better than others. Being born with a propensity toward desiring virtue, some can choose and do courageous acts and become courageous, and so morally virtuous. In contrast, others cannot. But one can't be morally responsible for what lies beyond one's power to control (Pereboom 2001). We can still praise courage and the courageous. But if people are not morally responsible for being less eligible for such praise, it is unfair and wrong to hold that being less virtuous than others renders it a matter of lesser moral urgency to facilitate greater well-being gains for those with the misfortune to be less virtuous. The claim then is that being more or less deserving in a way that renders it morally more or less valuable that one fare well in life (have high well-being) comes about only in ways that lie within one's power to control.

Appeal here is to the control principle: one can be morally responsible for something, and hence liable to being judged morally praiseworthy or blameworthy depending on its quality, only if the thing lies within one's power to control. And continuity suggests a companion principle: the harder and more painful it would be to understand what morality calls on one to choose and do, then adjusting for the stakes, the greater the moral credit that accrues to one if one successfully tries to do that and the less the moral discredit that accrues to one if one does not.

Reply: Deservingness as Conscientious Effort

There is a fork in the road here. On one path, one dismisses the control principle, and affirms an account of moral deservingness such as a quality of will account that allows that one can become morally deserving in ways beyond one's power to control. The more you succeed in doing what is actually morally right, for the reasons that make it right, the more virtuous, and hence the more morally deserving you are – whether or not your becoming virtuous lay within your power to control (Arpaly 2002).

But another path also beckons, which rebels at this elitist thought. On this path, we say that being equally persons, all of us must equally be able to become morally deserving. Roughly, insofar as each of us sincerely tries to figure out what is right and conform her will to that, she becomes morally deserving, regardless of success that reflects differential ability rather than differential effort. We seek to develop an account of moral deservingness that accepts the control principle. Here's a start at an attempt.

Figuring out what is right to do and doing it might be beyond one's power to control. But one can make conscientious efforts to do that, and so make oneself morally deserving. Being a person, one will confront the moral question: what do I owe to others by way of consideration and treatment? *Deservingness, first pass:* the more one tries to dispose one's will toward identifying what one morally owes to others and doing that, the more deserving one is. But making such conscientious effort might be pointless. One knows one cannot identify what is right to do, or if one knew, one could not do it. So back to the drawing board: *Deservingness, second pass.* As just previously stated, but add: the conscientious agent makes efforts to learn what is morally right to the degree she thinks doing so is appropriate (sensible), and she makes efforts to bring it about that she conforms to what is morally right by her lights to the degree she thinks doing so is sensible, appropriate. Also, she tries (to the extent she thinks appropriate) to bring it about that her beliefs about appropriateness are correct, and so on. (There is a regress here; harmless I hope.) – But obviously people will differ in their native traits and propensities, given them beyond their power to control, that affect the degree to which they become deserving by the second pass formulation. So make another revision. *Deservingness, third pass:* the determination of how morally praiseworthy/blameworthy a person is proceeds in two stages. At stage one, the extent to which the person exhibits conscientiousness (second pass) is assessed. This yields a raw conscientiousness score. Each person's raw conscientiousness score is then adjusted to reflect appropriately the ways in which the circumstances of each agent, beyond her power to control, affect her level of conscientiousness actually exhibited. This yields (notionally, we can't accurately see into people's souls) the true conscientiousness score. Compare to ideal handicapping of golfers for a tournament so that any golfer of any ability and facing whatever particular obstacles to a good game afflict her that day, has the same opportunity to win.

Deservingness as conscientious effort obviously will have highly revisionary implications for commonsense understandings of who is more morally deserving, who less. The upstanding bourgeois citizen with slight moral faults might be almost faultless in ways beyond her power to control, and therefore is hardly morally deserving at all; the serial ax murderer may be morally praiseworthy by virtue of struggling immensely to do right. These revisionary implications might be acceptable on reflection.

3.2.5 Objection: Double Prioritarianism Has Perverse Implications

Suppose that Robinson Crusoe is living out his life isolated on a desert island. None of the actions he can take would have any impact on the lives of anyone other than himself. Near the end of his life, he faces a choice between just two courses of action. He could take steps to improve his moral character, rendering himself more deserving. The alternative course of action is to forgo attempts at character development and instead drink the bottle of tequila he has just discovered while basking in the sun and enjoying the sunset. The second course of action would increase his lifetime well-being by a greater amount but the first, by increasing his lifetime deservingness score, would increase the moral value of the lesser amount of well-being that would accrue to him on this life path. Depending on the specific numbers in the specific instance, desert-catering prioritarianism seems liable to grind out the implication that the priority-weighted moral value of the well-being he gains in the first course of action is greater than the priority-weighted moral value of the well-being gains that the second course of action would deliver. So the character improvement course of action is the one he ought to select. This could hold, it seems, even if there is zero chance that he will ever get an opportunity to put his new moral character into action, because no such decision problems will arise. This judgment seems off-base, and condemns the moral view that implies it.

Here is another version of the same underlying issue. Suppose there is unfortunately nothing we can do to prevent Carmen, near death, from suffering a huge well-being loss. We cannot cut short her life or otherwise prevent her well-being loss. But suppose we can bring it about that she orients her will toward evil, becomes less deserving, and hence her impending welfare loss comes to have lesser moral disvalue. As with Robinson, it is certain that no effect on any decision she makes will arise via the reorientation of her will. She will have no opportunity to have any further impact on anyone's life. Still, if the numbers are in a certain range, double priority implies that we ought to strive to bring it about that Carmen becomes less morally deserving, thereby reducing the moral disvalue of her inevitable coming welfare loss. Let it be the case that her entire life has been grim, so she has lifetime negative well-being, the moral disvalue of which will lessen with her prospective lowered moral deservingness score. (Here we assume the measure of well-being has a nonarbitrary zero point, below which living that life is worse than never having lived at all.) So we ought to be seeking to corrupt Carmen's moral character. But this seems a crazy suggestion.

Replies:

No One Can Affect Another's True Deservingness

One possible reply would, it might seem, partially extinguish the objection. This reply says that if you accept the control principle, you should deny that one person's acting to generate a causal force that pushes another person toward blameworthy orientation of her will can ever affect that person's all things considered adjusted assessment of her deservingness. The causal push just becomes another component of the agent's circumstances, which make it harder or easier, and more painful or pleasant, for the individual to orient her will properly. But a final assessment of someone's deservingness should fully register the effect of this ensemble of circumstances, and be adjusted to offset their impact. If no one can ever affect how truly deserving anyone besides oneself becomes, then at least the Carmen-type puzzle cases do not arise.

This reply fails. Of course, if one brings it about that the agent whose deservingness one is trying to alter is determined by one's intervention to shift the orientation of her will, if it is beyond her power to control how she responds to the situation with intervention, then she can't be responsible for any resultant shift. But one's intervention might raise the chances that the target agent will shift orientation, without leaving the agent no wiggle room for an exercise of her will. So someone could act toward me, seeking to bring it about that I become corrupt, and increasing the chance that will occur, without eliminating my responsibility for allowing my will to orient one way or another. The intervention alters the opportunity for me to try conscientiously or not, and to what degree, but still leaves me with an opportunity, to which I might respond in a more or less creditable way. This holds also if the person who intervenes, affecting one's opportunity later to become more or less deserving, is oneself. So although this terrain is murky, we should accept that people can act intentionally and unintentionally in ways that can affect the likelihood that another person will become more deserving or less. (Accepting this is acknowledging that moral luck is not completely eliminable in human life.)

It Is in Itself, All Else Equal, a Better World, Impartially Assessed, if People Are More Deserving

One possible response is further to amend prioritarianism to allow that someone's becoming more morally deserving in itself makes outcomes better. It's a better world, all else equal, when people are more morally deserving rather than less. The discussion in this section has already anticipated and accepted this suggestion. It helps, a bit, with the problem at hand. So there are two effects when we facilitate Carmen's becoming more deserving. She becomes more morally deserving, which we are supposing is in itself morally valuable, and the moral disvalue of her having inexorably a hellish life of negative well-being increases. The first effect may offset the second. But it seems there will still be cases where by the numbers the second effect determines the overall value judgment, and this might still seem counterintuitive. Double priority can yield odd judgments.

Further Examples Take Away the Sting of the Robinson and Carmen Puzzles

Perhaps what drives the thought that the deservingness prioritarian judgment on the Carmen example is counterintuitive is a deontological thought, one should not strive to worsen anyone's character, at least when that brings about no welfare gain. Suppose Carmen intends wrongfully to harm some innocents, and by tempting her to become greedier (and more undeserving), her extra greed would somehow cause her plan to harm innocents to go awry, resulting in harm to her, not the innocents. In this case the fact that the moral disvalue of the well-being loss that will independently befall Carmen is somewhat lessened by her lessened moral deservingness does seem to be a consideration weighing in favor of tempting her. So maybe there is some special feature of the particular original Carmen example, and something else special about the Robinson worry, that make them explicable without undermining the conviction, priority should go to the deserving.

One possibility is that aiming to corrupt original Carmen's character, to render it less impartially bad that she suffers an inevitable well-being loss that is about to hit her, is bad for Carmen, because living a life that is good for one from a prudential standpoint includes responding appropriately to the duty one has to have due consideration for others. So in the circumstances as specified, trying to corrupt Carmen's character, if the attempt succeeds, is making her life go even worse for her that it was otherwise going to go, given the big harm looming over her and unavoidably about to strike her. Other things equal, being oriented to evil and dying a gruesome death are worse, from the prudential standpoint, than being oriented to good and dying a gruesome death.

This is an issue about the nature of well-being, touched on in the Victor Tadros anecdote about young Genghis Khan mentioned in Section 1. If our response to Carmen's looming miserable fate is so to speak to twist the knife, to make her lifetime well-being even lower, that effect surely outweighs the impartial consideration that if a harm must fall on someone, other things equal, this bad event is less bad, the less deserving she is. I have expressed disagreement with this moralized view of well-being. I tend to think a gangster who pays no heed to conscience can live a great life, enviable in prudential terms, though of course it is *morally* bad that the gangster is so morally nasty. But I have offered no argument supporting this claim. And we should recognize that if the moralized idea if well-being is correct, then the claim that we ought not to try to corrupt Carmen's character in the original Carmen decision problem coheres perfectly well with priority for the deserving. Moreover, we should accept that if the moralized view of well-being is incorrect, our confused intuitive feeling that it is correct might explain our reaction to the example – so definitely giving up the moralized view should explain away our strong response that in the original Carmen example priority for the deserving implies a wrong judgment about what to do.

Another possible response is to deny that striving to change the orientation of one's will, in the direction of greater conscientiousness, when one knows for sure that doing this will never result in one's making morally better choices and acting better, renders one more deserving. Pointless striving is, well, pointless. If Robinson's and Carmen's strivings to orient their wills aright are pointless and known to be pointless, then they are not making themselves more morally deserving by such striving. On this view, striving to dispose oneself to identify what is right and do it enhances deservingness, and is in itself morally valuable, conditional on the striving not being pointless.

But why is striving purely to make one's will better not in itself morally valuable, so not pointless? We acknowledged, it's a better world, all else equal, when people are more rather than less deserving. The response is that orienting one's will in a way one knows is inapt – has no chance of doing anyone any good – is not becoming more deserving. Becoming more deserving is good in itself, impersonally, even if not good for the agent whose deservingness score rises. But if Robinson understands what he would be doing – and he should be trying to understand correctly – he will see that pointless striving is not deservingness enhancing.

We end up with the view that people's becoming more rather than less deserving is in itself a morally valuable feature of an outcome, as is people's gaining more rather than less well-being. Moreover, the moral value of well-being gains for people is amplified or diminished by double priority weighting.

This doctrine looks promising, at least if the problem flagged by the Robinson and Carmen examples can be defused in one way or another. Notice that this problem arises for double prioritarianism, whether the view is developed by adopting a conception of deservingness that satisfies, or one that dismisses, the control principle.

Can Doing the Morally Right Act for the Right Reasons Thereby Make One Undeserving?

In passing, it may be worth flagging another puzzle. Suppose your neighborhood is being menaced by a bully. The police are no help. You can deter the bully only by credibly threatening excessive violence against the bully if he does not desist. And you can only make your threat credible by actually disposing your will conditionally, to respond with excessive and wrongful force if the bully does not comply with the threat. For sure, the result will be the best result, the bully desists. But your will is corrupted, to a degree – bent on engaging in immoral violence if your threat is unsuccessful. So by doing what is morally right (issuing the threat), you thereby render yourself morally undeserving?

Gregory Kavka (1978) provides a high-stakes version of this example. He suggests it might be the case, in some situations in which nuclear superpowers confront one another, that credibly threatening massive retaliation against a nation that unleashes on one's country a nuclear first strike, is the only way to prevent great evils. And if the only way to make one's threat credible is actually to dispose one's will to massive retaliation, then doing what is morally right (making the threat that brings about very great good consequences) thereby brings it about that one is horribly blameworthy by being conditionally disposed to murder millions of people by a nuclear counterstrike, The problem case can arise, whether one accepts consequentialism or a nonconsequentialist nonabsolutist deontology. Kavka discerns a paradox here.

In the Kavka decision problem, one has two choices: (1) dispose one's will here and now to do the right thing, which will with high probability bring about enormous good and as a side effect disposes one to doing horrible evil if a very unlikely scenario arises, or (2) decline to dispose one's will in this way here and now, thereby avoiding the side effect bad disposition for the unlikely future. I suggest, in this decision problem, if the act of issuing the threat is right (in its expected consequences), one orients one's will better all things considered if one opts for choice (1), so becomes more deserving by opting for (1) rather than (2). Of course, if the bad future arises, one will then be faced with another choice, to carry out horribly disproportionate retaliation or not. In this second decision problem one will have the disadvantage that one's will is already oriented strongly toward the wrong choice. But being disposed however strongly to do X if situation Z arises does not determine for sure that one will do X if situation Z arises. One has some capacity, maybe slight, to reorient one's will in that scenario and do the right thing. And even if one fails to reorient, one's conscientious efforts to do this, adjusted to reflect the difficulty of making them, may render one morally deserving even if one ends up choosing horribly wrongly, and retaliates. Of course, doing the expectably right thing by issuing the conditionally wrongful threat may actually lead to one's threat not being successful and one's power to resist the temptation to retaliate horribly not being strong enough to prevent horrible retaliation. In that case, by the criterion of actual consequences, what one does, issuing in conditional excessive force, turns out wrong. But one's action remains expectably right. The situation is odd and morally troublesome, no doubt. But I but I do not see that a sensible deservingness priority view implies contradictory claims. There is no paradox looming.

3.3 Further Issues

3.3.1 Does the Control Principle Extinguish Moral Responsibility Altogether?

There is this further issue: Is the control principle compatible with any positive affirmation of moral responsibility and so people's being variously morally deserving? This is left an open question. No stand is taken on it in this discussion. So the prioritarian who accepts deservingness as a priority factor should be interpreted as saying, if people can be more or less morally deserving, then their degrees of moral deservingness affect the moral value of the welfare gains and losses that accrue to them. The prioritarian position I am describing is committed to the truth of this conditional not the truth of its antecedent clause. Maybe all human choices are deterministically caused events, for which the chooser cannot be morally responsible. But if either (1) compatibilism (determinism and moral responsibility are compatible) or (2) so-called free will libertarianism (determinism and moral responsibility are incompatible and human persons have free will) is true, there is room for moral deservingness to play a role in moral doctrines including prioritarianism.

3.3.2 Well-Being Gains as a Fitting Response to Deservingness

As already noted, a priority view to have determinate content must specify the temporal unit of the prioritarian concern. If one should give priority to helping someone, the worse off the person is, one needs to know – worse off as assessed over what stretch of time? The unit could be the moment at which the mooted help would accrue to the person, a stage or period of the person's life, or the person's entire lifetime. I have affirmed taking the lifetime to be the relevant temporal unit. The same question arises for the proposal to give priority to helping someone, the more morally deserving she is. I shall tentatively suggest that the person's lifetime deservingness is the relevant temporal unit.

Suppose you could bring it about that a welfare gain accrues to Sally or instead an identical gain to Sue. Recently, Sue has been exemplary in her efforts to do the right thing; her adjusted recent conscientiousness score is very high. In this respect Sarah has been laggard for years; her adjusted recent conscientiousness score is shamefully bad. But her stellar virtuousness during adolescence more than offsets her long slow moral slide downward since then. In lifetime desert terms, Sarah is more morally deserving.

The judgment that a welfare gain that could be channeled either to Sarah or Sally in this example, ought to go to Sarah, all else equal, on the ground that her lifetime deservingness is greater, is controversial even among those who agree that deservingness renders a person apt especially apt for welfare boosts. Dennis McKerlie writes:

> Suppose an idealistic reformer succeeds at the cost of great personal unhappiness, in overthrowing a corrupt regime. Once in power he becomes as cynical and oppressive as the dictator he replaced. Is it just if he experiences great happiness as a tyrant so that his lifetime happiness will match his lifetime virtue? Perhaps we want virtuous people to be happy while they are virtuous (McKerlie 2001, 274–275).

Given the instrumental confounds woven into the example, I suggest it has limited probative force against the lifetime perspective. But I have no argument against a reader who flatly disagrees.

There are several alternatives to the simple lifetime deservingness view that could stand as rivals to it. One is to weight a person's deservingness scores more heavily, the closer they are to the present. Another view would hold that your contemporaneous deservingness score increases the moral value of obtaining a welfare benefit for you at that very time: we should reward the virtuous when they are virtuous (and punish the vicious when they are vicious). Another view would have both an individual's lifetime deservingness score and her contemporaneous deservingness score combine to determine the intrinsic moral value of obtaining for this individual a welfare gain.

Another possibility: deservingness might be deemed to be situation-specific. Illustrating the idea that it is intrinsically morally valuable that people fare in welfare according to their moral deservingness, Shelly Kagan (2012) imagines that two miners are trapped and in peril after an explosion in a mine. We can rescue only one of the two. He observes that if we discover that one is seriously morally to blame for the peril both face, we should choose to rescue the blameless miner. Although Kagan himself accepts a lifetime perspective, the example will suggest to some readers a quite different approach. One could deny that the miners' deservingness or undeservingness that is not causally or in some other way closely related to their current predicament has any bearing on the question, which one if either is morally more eligible for rescue. In the same spirit, one might hold that my moral faults as a teacher do not affect the moral value of my gaining well-being increases in the different context of my relations with friends. Again, the lifetime perspective advocate will point out that the example as described suggests instrumental benefits would accrue from saving the innocent miner, and if one abstracts from these (here irrelevant) reasons, the lifetime perspective again appears plausible, despite our situation-specific judgment inclinations.

3.3.3 Generic Deservingness

Stepping back from the control principle, its plausibility and what might follow from it, one should note that the idea that it is morally desirable that good fortune in the quality of the life one enjoys should go by preference to the deserving more than to the undeserving is a generic claim that can be interpreted in various ways. That well-being increases are morally more valuable, all else equal, the more deserving the person who gains the well-being boost, can be affirmed independently of having determined what conception of deservingness is best. To be sensible, the affirmation must be accompanied by the proviso that further inquiry will eventually single out a plausible best conception of deservingness all things considered. Should that proviso turn out false, the sensible advocate of deservingness should give up the faith.

3.3.4 Practical Upshot

Some readers may find it implausible that considerations of moral deservingness could or should play any role in public policy formation or any practical choice of action. It's one thing to say, for example, sick people deserve health care. It is quite another to say that laws and public policies should be shaped by judgments about how morally worthy or unworthy individual citizens are. There could be no sensible evidence that would suit for guidance of such judgments. A decent society avoids basing public policy on such considerations. Any steps to move in this direction would involve the state in illiberal intrusions on individual freedoms that society ought to safeguard. These are reasonable concerns.

In reply, it is just as true that no state or social agency could base policies on fine-grained judgments of individual people's well-being levels and prospects.

Nonetheless, state policies and institutions ought to be concerned to promote individual well-being in fair ways. Even if the state should lack and does lack information needed to make judgments such as that Sam is morally more deserving than Sally, the state might be able indirectly to promote the channeling of well-being toward the deserving. The state might promote proxy indicators of deservingness. The state might place people in decision problems such that the morally more worthy will tend to choose better and fare better than others.

The extent to which justifiable state policies will pay heed to moral deservingness considerations depends on whether empirical conditions given the best understanding of deservingness enable such policies to succeed. If any available deservingness-catering policies would be counterproductive or would not pass a morally sensitive cost and benefit assessment, such policies should not be pursued. The extent to which a liberal affirmation of wide individual freedom is compatible with deservingness-catering policies is, I believe, an open question. No doubt many desert-catering policies would be immoral, indecent and illiberal, but the question is whether there are identifiable such policies that would be liberal and decent, or anyway justifiable all things considered.

Even if the answer to this question were negative, that would not block affirmation of priority for the deserving from having practical import by affecting what it is morally right and wrong to do. Catering to deservingness might be feasible for individuals to do, and pro tanto a duty for them, even if desert-catering at the level of state policy proved to be unfeasible.

3.3.5 Desert-Catering Is a Module That Could Be Attached to Other Views

This section has explored how priority could be modified so as to be responsive to deservingness. But notice, rivals to priority could similarly be modified to accommodate deservingness. We could opt for desert-catering egalitarianism, or desert-catering sufficientarianism, or even desert-catering utilitarianism. So the question, should our moral view be modified to be desert-catering, looks to be neutral in its bearing on the different question, should our outcome evaluation standard be prioritarian, or egalitarian, or utilitarian, or sufficientarian, or something else entirely.

4 Utilitarianism, Sufficiency, and Leximin

Further understanding of prioritarianism, in axiology and in the theory of morally right action, may be gained by comparing this doctrine to its prominent currently identified rivals. These include utilitarianism, sufficientarianism, egalitarianism, and the leximin version of egalitarianism. This section attempts some discussion of utilitarianism and also considers sufficiency and leximin together (as they share rejection of a continuity condition on acceptable principles). Continuous egalitarianism is explored in Section 5.

4.1 Utilitarianism

As a standard of outcome evaluation, utilitarianism holds that one outcome is better than another just in case the aggregate of utility summed across individual persons is larger in the first than in the second. To determine the aggregate utility in an outcome, add together the utility of each person in that outcome. Do the same for each outcome being compared. The outcome associated with the largest number (or the smallest if all the sums are negative numbers) is better than each of the others. This addition procedure assumes that the utility gains and losses of individual persons can be interpersonally cardinally compared. Utility is a measure of welfare (or well-being), how an individual's life is going for that very person. Welfare is whatever a person seeks insofar as she is prudent.

As a criterion of morally right action (what is morally required, what one ought to do), utilitarianism (i.e., act utilitarianism) combines act consequentialism (one morally ought always to do whatever would bring about the best outcome of any action available for choice) and the utilitarian standard for ranking outcomes as better or worse. Utilitarianism ranks outcomes and actions when the same individuals exist in the outcomes being compared, when different individuals but the same number of individuals exist, and when different individuals along with different numbers of individuals exist across the outcomes being compared.

There will be different versions of utilitarianism, each one filling in the content of *welfare* in the formulation of the doctrine with a different conception of what constitutes the welfare of individual persons. To give utilitarianism, or for that matter its close cousin prioritarianism, a fair hearing, one should fill in this blank with the most plausible conception of individual welfare one can identify.

Utilitarianism contains an idea of what it is to treat people equally, fairly and impartially. One counts each person's same-sized gain or loss of welfare exactly the same in the determination of the overall goodness of outcomes. "Everybody to count for one, nobody for more than one." A violation of equal counting would occur if, for example, one double-counted the welfare of oneself and one's family or clan members, or of members of a particular nation state, or those with a particular skin color or ancestry, or those of a favored caste or class, or men and not women, in calculating the goodness of outcomes.

The prioritarian accepts a different idea of what it is to treat people equally, fairly, and impartially. If we set aside for now variable-population comparisons we find the disagreement between utilitarianism and prioritarianism amounts to just this: the prioritarian accepts Pigou–Dalton and the utilitarian rejects that and instead affirms a principle that Krister Byqvist calls "Transactional Equity" (Byqvist 2014): a change that consists in reducing some individual's well-being by any amount k and also increasing by in the aggregate that same amount other individuals' well-being and does nothing else makes the resulting outcome equally good. To revert to the example introduced in Section 1, bringing about a one-unit well-being loss for homeless badly off Dolores and also an identical well-being gain for immensely well-off Felicity, or the reverse, would bring about equally good outcomes. The prioritarian advocate plants her flag in the sand on this point. The judgment that Pigou–Dalton is correct and transactional equity incorrect is a rock-bottom prioritarian commitment.

4.1.1 Fair Chances?

Despite the disagreement, prioritarianism and utilitarianism have deep affinities. Consider each outcome evaluation rule yoked to an act consequentialist criterion of morally right and wrong action. Priority is open to an objection made by Peter Diamond against utilitarianism (Diamond, 1967; see also Parfit 2012). Suppose we have an indivisible good (or bad) that must go to one of two persons who are identical in all respects relevant to their eligibility for receipt of the good (or bad). We can choose among just two courses of action: either (1) assign each of the two an equal chance of getting the good, as by a fair coin flip, followed by the allocation of the good to the one selected by the procedure or (2) just allocate the good to one or the other of the two. Utilitarianism judges the two actions equally permissible, and prioritarianism does so as well. As Diamond observes, to many, this judgment seems unfair. The same taint of unfairness attaches to utilitarianism and prioritarianism construed just as rules for outcome evaluation.

A utilitarian response, which might be pressed by the prioritarian as well, insists that the example relies on the assumption that having a chance of a good does not in itself boost well-being. Deny that assumption and the objection disappears. If getting an equal chance of a good followed by not getting it is better for one than simply not getting the good, the utilitarian has a basis for favoring the fair procedure over the brute allocation that sidesteps the fair procedure.

An alternative response would allow that from an ex ante perspective, before the outcome of the coin flip is known, having the chance of getting the good is a benefit, for which a prudent individual should be willing to sacrifice some good. But from an ex post perspective, when uncertainty is resolved, having had the chance is no benefit at all. If morality requires adopting an ex post perspective, one can discern no difference in one's well-being between the situation in which one has the chance followed by not getting the good and the situation in which one simply does not get the good. If so, it's not a black mark against the utilitarian that she will find no moral difference in the outcome that results from opting for the fair procedure and the outcome that results from eschewing it. Mutatis mutandis, the same holds for the prioritarian.

Consider a simple variation of the Diamond example. There are two stages of decision. Stage 1 is the same as the Diamond example. Then a new decision problem arises, in which one must allocate an indivisible good to one of three persons, two of whom were the recipients in the stage 1 problem. The third person is identical in all respects relevant to eligibility for the good as the first two; the only differences between persons are the differences in their well-being levels induced by the stage 1 problem. If having a chance at getting a good is itself a good, there would seem to be an argument for allocating the new good to the third person rather than to either of the other two. The person who won the stage 1 coin flip and got the good is now less eligible for receipt of the new benefit; that person is better off than the others. The person who had the chance of getting the good but did not get it is, it would seem, better off than the third person who did not have this chance but is otherwise relevantly the same in all eligibility respects. In prioritarian accounting, the third person is now worse off than this one who had the chance, and the outcome in which this third person gets the indivisible good is morally more valuable than an outcome in which the person who had a chance of getting the prior good but did not actually get it now receives the indivisible good in this subsequent decision problem.

If this seems counterintuitive or even bizarre, the problem is the assumption that a chance of getting a good is some lesser kind of good. Suppose we say instead that fairness involves the distribution of goods and bads across persons and also the distribution of chances of accruing these. Fair distribution across time then requires not only keeping track of good and bad receipt but also of each person's accrued chances that never materialized as goods or bads. For another example, suppose one has an indivisible bad that must be allocated to one of two persons, identical in all respects relevant to eligibility for the bad, except that one previously suffered a 99 per cent chance of instant death, but did not suffer death or any other actual harm. The imposition of the big chance of instant death was unknown to the individual. The prioritarian can say that the accumulated history of such chances that never materialized as actual good or bad is irrelevant to the fair treatment of individuals going forward.

In discussing the Diamond objection, we have moved from outcome evaluation to evaluation of prospects. Consider the well-studied case in which, for any proper action one might choose, one can identify the mutually exclusive and exhaustive outcomes to which the action might give rise, and associate with each of these possible outcomes the probability it will occur given one chooses this action, and also identify the value of each outcome should it occur. In choosing an action one is then choosing not a definite outcome but this array of possible outcomes the action might deliver. Choice of an action is in these circumstances choice of a prospect. In this situation a prominent rule for prospect evaluation and choice is to maximize expected utility. For each act one might choose, multiply the value of each possible outcome of that act times the probability it will occur if one chooses that act, sum the results for each act available for choice, and select the act with the highest sum. Choosing this act maximizes expected utility. Standard decision theory says one should evaluate prospects according to their expected utility (value). In our context, we identify utility with well-being. Utilitarianism then says, facing prospects, maximize the sum of expected well-being, and in the case in which each choice of a possible action yields an outcome for sure, maximize the sum of well-being.

4.1.2 Priority for Prospects

How should we extend priority to the evaluation of prospects? There are several options; I shall describe two. One extension says, one prospect is morally better than another just in case it contains a greater sum of priority-weighted ex ante expected well-being. On this view, to determine the moral value of a prospect, add up the priority-weighted ex ante expected well-being of each person facing the possible outcomes in that prospect. The prospect that affords the highest priority-weighted ex ante expected well-being total is the best prospect. On this view, each person's expected well-being in a prospect has diminishing marginal moral value (an addition to someone's expected well-being is more morally valuable, the lower the person's expected well-being would otherwise be). An alternative extension says, one prospect is morally better than another just in case it contains a greater sum of expected priority-weighted ex post well-being. On this view, to determine the moral value of a prospect, for each of its possible outcomes, add up the priority-weighted moral value of the well-being each person gets in that outcome, and multiply that sum times the probability that outcome will occur. Add up these numbers for all the possible outcomes of that prospect. The prospect with the highest number is the morally best prospect.

To see the difference between the two rules, suppose we could bring about either Prospect #1 or Prospect #2. What outcomes will ensue depends upon whether state of nature S1 or S2 obtains. Each of S1 and S2 has probability .5.

There are two persons, Sam and Sally. Each is equally well-off, apart from the outcomes of S1 and S2.

	Prospect #1		Prospect #2		
	S1	**S2**	**S1**	**S2**	**(S1 and S2 equiprobable)**
Sam	5	5	10.1	0	
Sally	5	5	0	10.1	,

The expected well-being for both individuals is higher under Prospect #2, so according to priority-weighted ex ante expected well-being, Prospect #2 has to be morally better than Prospect #1. But the outcome in Prospect #1 has greater priority-weighted well-being (we can suppose, given any of many plausible priority weightings). Ex ante prioritarian prospect evaluation judges Prospect #2 better and ex post prioritarian prospect evaluation judges Prospect #1 morally better. Ex ante prioritarian prospect evaluation incorporates each individual's prudential expected well-being into the prioritarian calculation of which prospect is best; ex post prioritarian prospect evaluation does not.

The ex post rule conflicts with Pareto for prospects. This Pareto condition says that if someone has higher expected well-being in one prospect, compared to a second, and no one in the first prospect has lower expected well-being in the second, the first prospect is superior to the second. Each of Sam's and Sally's expected well-being is higher under Prospect #2. But in endorsing that prospect, Pareto for prospects endorses as superior a prospect that we know in advance will bring about a morally worse outcome ex post, after uncertainty is resolved, as judged by priority-weighted outcome evaluation. How can that be sensible? Perhaps prioritarians are better advised to say, once we see this conflict, we should accept the ex post rule and reject Pareto for prospects (Adler 2012, Adler and Holtug 2019, Rabinowicz 2002, but for an opposed view, see Vallentyne 2013 and Otsuka and Voorhoeve 2018).

4.1.3 Value and Moral Value: A Sensible Distinction?

In a critical discussion of prioritarianism, John Broome (1991 and 2015) notes that the prioritarian outcome assessment distinguishes between (1) the well-being gain or loss that an individual stands to get in some outcome an agent might be able to bring about and (2) the moral value of that well-being gain or loss. He challenges whether this distinction makes sense. How can there be two different registrations of the individual's well-being gain or loss? For the utilitarian, there is just the one thing.

In reply, the distinction between how well your life is going for you and the moral value of your life going well to that degree is not a technical abstraction devised to serve some theoretical purpose. It's a distinction we appeal to in ordinary judgment. For example, reading a thorough biography of a Mafia boss, one might have good rough grounds for holding that by luck and cunning his life has gone very well for him, by any sensible measure. He enjoys lots of what anyone would identify as key components of a good life – good for the one who is living it. But it's another question, whether it is from the moral standpoint a good thing that his life is so good. A harsh moralist might insist that it would be intrinsically a good thing, quite apart from any further consequences, if the Mafia boss encountered terrible misfortune that rendered his life overall hellish in quality. Whether we agree or disagree, we understand what is being said. Common sense can be mistaken and confused, so we should be open to the possibility that this is so in this case. But the burden of proof lies with the skeptic. The utilitarian happens to have a moral theory such that, as common sense would put it, the true moral value of someone's welfare summed over time just is the sum of that person's welfare, and the true moral value of the community members' welfare is just the sum of the welfare of the members. This is a substantial claim about true moral value, which would need to be supported by compelling argument. It can't be shown to be right just by flatly denying that there is any distinction between the amount of good in a person's life and the moral value of the person having that amount of good (Adler and Holtug 2019, also Rabinowicz 2002).

4.1.4 Harsanyi's Arguments

In the 1950s the economist John Harsanyi developed two arguments linking the normative theory of rational decision-making to the claim that a version of utilitarianism is the uniquely correct rational criterion of right and wrong conduct, what one morally ought to do. Both arguments (in effect) urge that prioritarian and egalitarian doctrines of outcome evaluation and of rational choice are deeply in conflict with uncontroversial constraints on moral choice that emerge when we consider choices under risk.

The interpretation and assessment of Harsanyi's arguments depend on technical decision theory considerations. Explicating mathematical decision theory is not a task this introductory survey of priority can undertake. Interested readers can consult the authors cited in this footnote for background and overview.[4] In what follows I try to convey the flavor of the issues involved by informal characterization.

---

[4] See Harsanyi 1953, 1955. For doubts that the Harsanyi framework could issue in a defense of (anything close to) utilitarianism, which requires cardinal interpersonal comparison of welfare to

In a 1955 essay Harsanyi presents a set of axioms as rational constraints on impartial rankings of prospects over social outcomes. The axioms significantly include an account of rational preference that enables us to determine, not just that an individual is better off in one condition or another, but by how much the individual is better off. The picture conveyed is that for a population of individuals, each of them ranking prospects by their expected utility for oneself, the corresponding rational impartial evaluation ranks outcomes by the total of their expected utilities summed over all these individuals' rankings. Very roughly, the axioms seem hard to reject, but if you accept them, by logic you are committed to acceptance of a moral principle that is in the utilitarian family of views and anyway rules out priority. If your choices violate the axioms, your choices cannot be represented as maximizing your expected utility, and it is claimed that there can be situations in which your choices will be guaranteed to render you worse off by your own lights than other choices you could make, no matter how risks unfold into outcomes.

Stepping back from the precise details of the Harsanyi argument, we can discern a simple basis for skepticism regarding it. Normative decision theory essentially insists that one's reasoning about what to do should overall be consistent and should be appropriately responsive to shifts in empirical facts and empirical probabilities. But the core building blocks of priority outcome assessment (here we are setting to the side the complications introduced by deservingness priority and double prioritarianism) are the Pareto norms including anonymity, Pigou–Dalton, separability, and a continuity assumption. These claims taken together are not latently inconsistent. Acting on them, when the outcomes of actions one might prefer are known for sure, will not lead the agent to inconsistency in action. One can say, insofar as bringing about better rather than worse outcomes ought to guide choice, one should be guided by the core priority components as just stated. If Pigou–Dalton is correct, and the utilitarian substitute transactional equity is false, it is prioritarianism not utilitarianism that correctly ranks outcomes as better or worse.

Accepting the ex post rule for the moral evaluation of prospects, we should reject Pareto for prospects (see Rabinowicz 2002). As we have just seen, it can be the case that everyone's expected well-being is higher under Prospect #2 than under Prospect #1, yet we can know that whatever state of nature turns out to obtain, ex post the outcome under Prospect #1 will yield a higher sum of

---

be stateable, see Sen 1975; Weymark 1991, 2005; Roemer 1996, and for replies, Broome 1991; Risse 2002; Greaves 2016. See also Fleurbaey 2010 for discussion of prospects for egalitarianism in the wake of Harsanyi-Broome. For an overview of standard decision theory, including its extension to the general case in which relevant probability information is patchy, incomplete, or nonexistent, see, for example, Bradley 2017 and the references cited therein.

priority-weighted well-being than Prospect #2. At least in the range of cases where this is so, priority extended to prospect evaluation must judge #1 morally better than #2.

If we had reason to believe that Pigou–Dalton as a condition on outcome evaluation was incoherent or implausible, we would have reason to align outcome evaluation with Pareto for prospects, and favor a prospect evaluation principle that judges Prospect #2 morally superior to Prospect #1 as the ex ante rule does. But confidence in Pigou–Dalton should push our judgment the other way. We have reason to hold that the morally correct outcome evaluation rule finds best the outcome with highest priority-weighted well-being. From this secure perch, we hold that it is a task for the logician/decision theorist to discover the correct rule for evaluation of prospects that is coherent with outcome evaluation under certainty. On this view Pigou–Dalton guides the completion of normative decision theory for choices under risk and uncertainty. (This is in effect to invoke the Insulation position discussed in section #5.)

Harsanyi, a fertile theorist, had earlier proposed a social contract argument (Harsanyi 1953; see Bykvist 2014). Suppose an individual is to choose principles to regulate a society that she is to inhabit. The individual is assumed to choose by maximizing her expected utility. That is, she aims to choose the principles, the operation of which will maximize her expected utility. However, she is constrained to choose in an impartial fashion by being forced to choose behind a veil of ignorance. The veil prevents the choosing individual from knowing which of the N members of society she is. She knows she has a 1/N chance of being any of the members of society. She knows that each of the N members of society ranks possible social outcomes in a way that can be represented as maximizing that member's expected utility. Against this background, the choosing individual maximizes her expected utility by choosing that society be regulated by maximizing the average of the sum of the expected utilities of the members of society. This last statement is not quite correct; what is actually shown is that the choosing individual chooses in a way that is close to utilitarianism in certain ways and ends up choosing a principle that is close to the principle that requires maximizing average utility across the members of society, and this "close to utilitarianism" outcome rules out prioritarian and egalitarian rival norms.

Discussing Harsanyi's social contract derivation of utilitarianism, which anticipates his own original position argument for the principles of justice he defends in the landmark *A Theory of Justice*, John Rawls (1999) comments that the fact that the average utilitarian principle and not maximize-the-total utilitarianism emerges from Harsanyi's endeavor shows something significant. The generic social contract idea is that justice consists in arranging society according to principles that free and equal persons would choose in a decision process that was fairly set up for the purpose of settling these fundamental terms of social cooperation. Average utilitarianism is a contender in the social contract arena; this doctrine can be given a plausible even if not ultimately correct social contract rationalization, whereas sum total utilitarianism cannot.

But actually it seems that the appeal of the average version of utilitarianism in the Harsanyi setup rests on a quirk of formulation, a tear in the veil of ignorance. The choosing individual knows that she will be a member of the society that she will be inhabiting. So she has no self-interested reason to favor the addition of new people into society unless the addition of people happens to boost the average utility. She knows a particular fact about herself that she can turn to her advantage. So the Harsanyi social contract seems an unsuitable framework for getting insight into population ethics, that will settle what morality requires by way of adding new people to the world.

A larger suspicion intrudes at this point. By adjusting the setup of the social contract construction, you control what its outcome will be – which principles will be selected. How should we set up the social contract? A skeptic will say, we should set it up in whatever way will bring about choice of correct principles, or if we don't know the correct principles, then whatever principles at present we have most independent moral reason to accept. On this view, the social contract construction is a showcase for displaying principles the social contract theorist finds plausible and not a device for identifying what is really true in matters of justice and morality.

Some respond to the Harsanyi-style social contract by noting that the idea of self-interested choice behind a veil of ignorance that imposes impartiality is too close to the basic idea of utilitarianism for this contract to serve as a justification of utilitarianism rather than an assertion of it (Roemer 2002; Adler 2012; Parfit 2012). The Harsanyi social contract gives no reason to reject (for example) the core egalitarian norm that egalitarians and prioritarians share: Pigou–Dalton.

The choosing individual in the Harsanyi social contract decision problem will have no reason to choose Pigou–Dalton or anything in the vicinity – but so what? You could after all modify the setup so that the choosing individual is risk-averse in utility. The prioritarian and egalitarian should be comrades in saying with one voice that self-interested choice behind a veil of ignorance that prevents you from specially advantaging yourself by the choice is not the correct statement of the decision problem – if indeed there is any such magical thing – the outcome of which necessarily constitutes the set of principles that morally bind our conduct and choice of policies.

4.2 Sufficiency Doctrines

The basic sufficientarian idea is that what matters morally is not whether everyone has the same or close to the same, nor whether the welfare sum or the priority-weighted welfare sum is maximized. What matters morally is that all people have enough or sufficient, measured by whatever the right standard is for judging whether distributive justice obtains in society. The just society has no humanly avoidable insufficiency (for objections, see Casal 2007).

The trick is to identify a plausible line of sufficiency. Why is it located here and not higher or lower? Intuitive ideas of how much good in a life is "enough" will vary wildly with circumstances. Think of trying to decide what is a sufficiently good life in a hunter-gatherer culture with inevitable low life expectancy and in a wealthy and harmonious society of the further future. In a welfarist framework, it is especially hard to come up with a compelling answer. The sufficiency threshold is supposed to make it the case that getting as many as possible just to the threshold is an urgent moral matter but that past the threshold, this special moral urgency of promoting well-being gains for people disappears. Roger Crisp (2003) interprets the sufficiency ideal as a hybrid, requiring priority for achieving gains for a person, the greater the shortfall between her present level and the sufficiency line, and utilitarianism for assessing the value of obtaining gains for people above the threshold. He associates this axiology with the sentiment of reasonable compassion, said to be triggered by people's being subthreshold.

The prioritarian partly agrees. In axiological terms, priority agrees with sufficiency that if better-off and worse-off persons are all already incredibly well-off, the gap between someone ten units higher in well-being and someone ten units lower matters less, than would be the case if worse offs were incredibly badly off. But a smaller reason is still a positive reason rather than no reason at all, and depending on circumstances, small reasons can make a large difference to moral assessment.

The prioritarian stance would be weakened if a compelling case could be made for attaching special moral importance to attaining a particular well-being level. Lacking a compelling argument for singling out a single welfare level (or band), the difficulty is not eased by raising or lowering the asserted threshold. Lowering the threshold makes it all the more implausible to deny that a welfare gain obtained for a person just above the threshold is morally more valuable than obtaining an identical gain for someone at a far higher above-threshold level. Raising the threshold diminishes the range of cases in which priority and hybrid sufficiency must disagree, but does not eliminate it entirely.

A sufficiency doctrine might float entirely outside a welfarist framework. The idea would be that the sufficient line to which all must have access is set by a standard that assesses people's condition in non-welfare terms. Some say that there should be sufficient opportunity for acting autonomously or functioning as an agent or achieving what one has reason to value.

4.3 Maximin and Leximin

Maximin says, maximize the advantage level of the worst-off person. Maximin is a combination of the norms of making people better off and of equalizing their condition that eschews leveling down entirely. It favors transfers of resources from better-off individuals to the worst off, until further transfers would not at all improve the condition of the worst off. But it never recommends transfers or other policies that would worsen the condition of any better-off person without improving the condition of the worst off. Here we consider versions of maximin and related views that assess the condition of individuals in terms of their welfare levels.

Maximin is silent on what to do when policies are available that would have no impact on the worst off but would affect the position of others in the population. As an axiology, it ranks outcomes by the condition of the worst-off member of society in that outcome, ignoring shifts in other people's condition (that do not plunge another into becoming worst off). This means that maximin is incompatible with the Pareto norms: a shift from a status quo to another outcome in which one or more persons who are not worst off become better off does not get assessed as an improvement by maximin. Leximin is maximin adjusted to be consistent with Pareto norms. It says, as a first priority, make the position of the worst off as good as possible, then as a second priority, make the position of the second worst-off person as good as possible, and so on, until, as a last priority, make the position of the very best off as good as possible.

Like sufficiency doctrines, maximin and leximin do not incorporate a continuity condition. (See Section 1 for an informal characterization of continuity.)

Incorporating continuity, priority consorts with the ideas that the values we should care about vary by degree and appropriately are traded off against each other. A loss falling on any one individual can in principle be compensated, at the morally set terms of trade, by gains for one or more others. Less of this can be offset by more of that or of those other things, so that the outcome with the loss and also with the appropriate combination of offsetting gains is not a worsening of the situation all things considered.

To illustrate this priority versus leximin conflict, think back to the simple example of channeling a benefit to an extremely badly off person Dolores or alternatively to an extremely well-off person Felicity. If I am Dolores, I might contemplate a range of outcomes. In each outcome, either I get one unit of welfare or instead Felicity gets X amount of welfare, which is always greater than one. As I imagine X getting bigger, at some point I should say, "It's not fair that I should grab so to speak a small trinket when the cost of my getting it is that Felicity loses some large jewel." Given that I am so badly off, some priority attaches to getting gains and preventing losses for me, but there is a limit, which I should recognize and accept, to this priority favoring. There is a reciprocity norm of a sort surfacing here. Each human life is special and we should care about its going well. Each person is special, but no one (however badly off) is so special as to warrant limitless forgoing of gain or acceptance of loss by better offs to help worse offs. "Be reasonable," we sometimes say, meaning that the person addressed should give up a small gain, or accept a small loss, when that would bring about sufficient gains for others. So understood, it's a plausible prescription.

5 Egalitarianism versus Prioritarianism

Objections to the priority view have been forcibly asserted by Michael Otsuka and Alex Voorhoeve (2009, 2018, also Otsuka 2015). A considerable literature has blossomed in response to their writings. Most contributors to this discussion concede a lot of ground to the Otsuka–Voorhoeve objections (e.g., Parfit 2012; Williams 2012; Weber 2014; Segall 2015).

This section like the preceding one sets aside the Section 2 assertion of double prioritarianism. I'm not withdrawing or hedging my affirmation of priority for the deserving, just simplifying the discussion. The two priority clams (for the worse off and for the deserving) are separate and independent.

Should we embrace prioritarianism or instead some form of egalitarianism (or neither)? Recall, the egalitarian holds that it is morally bad, unjust and unfair, if some are worse off than others. The doctrine admits of various views about how to measure degrees of inequality. The egalitarian will likely affirm that more equal distributions are better along with also affirming that outcomes in which people have more rather than less well-being are better. In contrast, the prioritarian holds that a benefit obtained for a person is morally more valuable, the worse off that person would otherwise be. Prioritarians and egalitarians are united in affirming Pigou–Dalton. By that affirmation, both doctrines favor more equal distributions.

They disagree on the abstract sounding condition of person separability. In other words, the prioritarian holds that it does not in itself morally matter how an individual's well-being condition compares to that of others. Getting a benefit for you when your lifetime well-being would otherwise be 10 is morally more valuable than your getting this benefit when your lifetime level would otherwise be 11. But the moral value of your getting this benefit does not vary depending on how others are faring. In contrast, for the egalitarian, the moral value of your getting this well-being gain varies, depending on whether others are better off or worse off. The prioritarian holds that the ranking of the moral value of outcomes depends only on the sum of individual priority-weighted well-being levels. The contribution that any one individual's condition makes to the overall moral evaluation of outcomes depends only on that very individual's weighted well-being total and not on any relation to any other individual's well-being. This strong separability insistence does not rule out that people's being more or less unequal in aspects of their condition may matter in itself or instrumentally by way of having an impact on some individuals' well-being levels.

How important is the moral disagreement between the prioritarian and the egalitarian? Marc Fleurbaey (2015) has urged that "any prioritarian will always find some egalitarian view [that is, some pluralist view valuing more welfare as well as more equal distribution of it] which reaches the same practical conclusion about all possible cases, although possibly for different reasons." So we seem to be looking at a tempest in a teapot. Clarification: by "all possible cases" Fleurbaey means cases of decision under certainty, or evaluation of outcomes that for sure will arise from chosen actions. Significant disagreement remains possible when evaluation of prospects is at issue.

It might seem puzzling how two views could disagree about justifying reasons for choice and yet come to the same verdicts regarding choice of actions and policies in all cases barring those involving risky and uncertain prospects. Won't the reasons that are disagreed about issue in opposed judgments about what outcome of those reachable would be best in some possible circumstances?

The answer is No. Notice that there is a logical relationship between holding that a welfare gain of a given size is more morally valuable if it goes to a person, the lower her well-being level, and holding that a welfare gain of that size is morally more valuable if the gain goes to someone at lower well-being level rather than to someone at a higher well-being level. Particular prioritarian weightings and particular egalitarian views can differ. But for any specific prioritarian weighting that fixes how much more valuable are gains, depending on how low is the well-being level of the potential recipient, there will correspond an egalitarian function that combines sensitivity to average or total level of well-being and a particular degree of inequality aversion, that yields the same ranking of reachable outcomes. To put it another way, although the prioritarian cares nothing for getting nearer to equality in itself, she must instrumentally value welfare preserving inequality reduction.

There is still room for serious disagreement, as recent debates have shown. The disagreement shows up when we consider choices when the action chosen might issue in different outcomes depending on how the world unfolds following the action. Choice of an action is in these circumstances choice of a prospect.

Facing choice among prospects, the egalitarian, like the prioritarian, might opt for any of various rules for prospect evaluation. When outcomes will for sure be worse by equality standards, after risks play out, the egalitarian might opt for ex post evaluation. But looking at one-person worlds, or situations in which only one person's interests matter, the egalitarian sees no equality issue, so has reason to embrace prospect evaluation by ex ante expected well-being, whereas the prioritarian taking an ex post perspective does not.

A prioritarian evaluates an outcome by the priority-weighted well-being summed across the persons in the outcome. The higher the priority-weighted well-being, the better the outcome. Facing choice among prospects, how should the prioritarian proceed? There is a question as to how to extend prioritarianism to the evaluation of prospects. There are several rival views. For the reason mentioned in the last section, I assume the best prioritarian proposal anchors to the outcomes that emerge when unfolding events have resolved uncertainty: One prospect is morally better than another just in case it contains a greater sum of expected priority-weighted ex post well-being. Priority coupled with act consequentialism then holds that the right action to choose and do is the one that maximizes probability-weighted ex post priority-weighted well-being.

Marching under this banner of separability, the prioritarian will hold that the priority-weighted evaluation of prospects will feed into moral evaluation in a one-person universe in exactly the same way as it would in a community of many persons or more generally a many-person universe. Priority-weighted evaluation of prospects applies to a Robinson Crusoe alone in the universe just as in a social setting.

This appearance invites the egalitarian objection that priority is wrongly insensitive to the unity of the individual and the separateness of persons. That is to say, when only one person's interests should be considered, or only several persons' interests that are rising and falling together in lockstep, prudential considerations should rule, meaning that it is at least permissible to fulfill any duty one has to help by maximizing the ex ante expected welfare of those who will be affected. For Otsuka and Voorhoeve, this idea of expected welfare is idealized; the relevant individual preferences are taken to be the self-interested preferences individuals would have after ideal deliberation with full relevant information; the measure of expected welfare is given by the Von-Neumann–Morgenstern axioms. Whatever the outcome that ensues, one has acted reasonably to help those affected. In contrast, when several persons' interests are involved, and might be in conflict, helping some might leave others behind, and doing what might help or hurt some might affect how their condition compares to that of still others with claims to comparative fairness. In such cases there is a shift in moral perspective, and considerations of interpersonal fairness are triggered, but priority pays no heed to the shift. This is the Otsuka and Voorhoeve (O and V) critique.

By way of illustration, consider a one-child version of the Nagel example introduced in Section 1. You must move either to the countryside or the city. The move is neutral for all persons who might be affected except a single child. If this child becomes disabled, she will be better off in the city. If she does not become disabled, she will be better off in the country. There is a .5 probability that she will become disabled and .5 probability that she will not. The welfare impact is as follows:

	Prospect #1 (Move to city)		Prospect #2 (Move to country)	
	S1 (disabled)	S2 (able)	S1 (disabled)	S2 (able)
Welfare of child	39	50	30	60

Assume you ought to act in whatever way is in the best interest of the child. What is that? Her expected well-being is slightly higher (in the example, 45) if you move to the country, and lower (44.5) if you move to the city. For some prioritarian weightings, the priority-weighted value to her of each possible outcome of choice times its probability is higher if you move to the city.

O and V say, it is at least morally permissible, and perhaps required, to maximize expected well-being here, as egalitarian views will allow. The outcome evaluation of the two prospects should favor Prospect #2. Denying this, prioritarian views go wrong.

In contrast, consider a two-child version of the one-child example just discussed. There are two children, one disabled, and assume again either that they are the only people there are or that morality permits ignoring the interests of everyone's interests but theirs. In the city for sure, and also in the country if rainy weather dominates, the outcome will be 50 for Able and 39 for Disabled. If the move to the country is accompanied by sunny weather, Able gets 60 and Disabled 30. There is a .5 chance of rainy weather and a .5 chance of sunny weather if the move to the country is made.

Prospect #1 Move to city		Prospect #2 Move to country	
Same outcome whether rainy or sunny		S1 (rainy)	S2 (sunny)
Able child	50	50	60
Disabled child	39	39	30

In the one-child example, there is a prudential justification for imposing a risky choice on the child. If things turn out badly, it remains the case that the chance this bad outcome would obtain for the child is the cost of bringing about for her a chance that she herself would benefit. We acted in your ex ante best interest, we might say. Otsuka and Voorhoeve also urge, in the one-child case there is no competing claim issue and in the two-child example, there is. It is harder to justify imposing a risk of loss on someone in the face of a competing claims objection.

A competing claims issue arises when an agent chooses between benefiting one person and benefiting another (Fleurbaey and Voorhoeve 2012). Here each has a claim to be benefited, and each one's claim is stronger, the larger the benefit she would get if the choice favors her, and the worse her baseline level of well-being, compared to the level of well-being of the other.

The egalitarianism O and V favor (also Buchak 2017) registers a shift in the two decision problems, in terms of prospect evaluation and choice of what should be done. O and V see moving to the country as the morally superior choice in the one-child example and moving to the city as morally superior in the two-child example choice. They object that priority goes wrong in failing to register the difference between the prudential choice problem and the competing claims problem. (Priority reaches the verdict that the move to the city is the right choice in both examples and for the same reason.)

A separate objection raised by O and V is that priority is insensitive to the moral value of equality.

This objection can be illustrated by a decision problem described by John Broome (1991, 2015) and discussed by Rabinowicz (2002), Fleurbaey (2015) and Otsuka and Voorhoeve (2018). Suppose there are two people in the universe, call them Meg and Nell, and a choice between two prospects for them would have the welfare outcomes listed in the following table. There are two possible states of the world, and a .5 probability of each possible state arising.

	Prospect #1		Prospect #2	
	S1	S2	S1	S2 (both states equiprobable)
Meg	1	2	1	2
Nell	1	2	2	1

Broome notes the utilitarian outcome evaluation ranking will regard choice of either prospect as equally good. In each prospect, ex ante expected well-being summed over all affected persons is the same. He supposes any egalitarian ranking will regard Prospect #1 as superior to #2. The egalitarian ranking will balance the aims of maximizing ex ante expected well-being and equalizing ex ante expected well-being and also equalizing final well-being. In terms of the first two desiderata, prospects #1 and #2 are equally good, and in terms of the third, Prospect #1 is superior. A priority ranking could conceivably reflect the ex ante priority-weighted prospects or the ex post priority-weighted final outcome sum or some mix of the two. In this Element, I have supposed the prioritarian opts for ex post priority-weighted final possible outcomes sum. But in this example the ex ante prospects and the ex post final possible outcomes sum yield the same ranking of prospects. So in this example utilitarianism and prioritarianism converge in judgment and equality differs.

With Broome, Otsuka and Voorhoeve note, Prospect #1 guarantees equal outcomes and Prospect #2 guarantees unequal outcomes. There is ex hypothesi nothing that differentiates the persons that could provide moral reason to favor one getting more than others. In this situation, if inequality is unjust and unfair, priority is tone-deaf to a significant moral consideration, registered by egalitarianism. Contrary to priority, Prospect #1 is morally superior to #2.

5.1 Discussion: Priority Strikes Back

The "ignores equality" objection just noted admits of a quick reply. The worry that the prioritarian wrongly dictates the same response to decision problems where prudential concerns alone matter and to other decision problems, raises harder issues, harder to settle.

5.1.1 Separability

Priority in the version under review here, a rule for outcome ranking, includes commitment to welfarism plus Pigou–Dalton, continuity, and person separability. Otsuka and Voorhoeve are targeting the extension of this doctrine to the evaluation of prospects. The "ignores equality" objection calls attention to the commitment to separability. Is this a problem?

Recall, separability in persons says that the moral value of one outcome, compared to another, is unaffected by the well-being levels of unaffected persons. If we extend separability to prospect evaluation, it says that the moral value of one complete prospect, compared to another, is unaffected by the well-being prospects of persons whose well-being prospects are unaffected. In choosing between Prospect #1 and #2, Meg's prospects are unaffected, they are equally good in #1 and #2. The same holds for Nell's prospects. Prospect separability rules out favoring #1 over #2 in that case. They are equally good. The fact that the composition of their prospects differs (Meg is better off in S1 than in S2, Nell the reverse) cannot, consistently with prospect separability, affect the comparative ranking of #1 and #2.

One natural interpretation of the judgment that Prospect #1 is superior to Prospect #2 is that it matters morally for its own sake and not merely instrumentally, how one person's condition compares to that of others. This is just what Parfit identifies as the defining difference between egalitarian and prioritarian approaches. In this light, it's hard to see objection 3 as an objection to priority; it's rather an emphatic statement by O and V that they disagree. Priority asserts what egalitarianism flatly denies.

To be sure one has one's eye on the genuine difference, one needs to filter out the distracting possible instrumental defects (or merits) of inequality. Perhaps when people's well-being levels differ, that causes resentment, bad feeling, mistrust, a disposition against productive cooperation, and so on. But these considerations are by the way. If they occur, that affects the well-being levels of the people in the population and we have a different decision problem.

5.1.2 The Unity of the Self and the Separateness of Persons

In response to the O and V critique, five responses will be offered. Each has advantages and disadvantages. The reader will have to judge which ones, if any, to endorse. Stepping back from details of the debate, I do not see a dramatic, compelling criticism of priority. The egalitarian critique calls attention to an interesting point. It is not so clear how to extend axiological priority from a standard for assessing outcomes to a standard for assessing lotteries over outcomes.

That said, the assertion of the "separateness of persons" slogan should not be deemed to establish any sort of presumptive case against priority, whether construed as axiology or as an impartial beneficence duty. The slogan can be used to rally us to different moral claims. The slogan challenges utilitarianism, which bids us to maximize aggregate welfare summed across persons, without registering norms of fair distribution of welfare across persons. But prioritarian doctrine registers fair distribution norms. The slogan also resonates with the different thought that each person has her own life to live, and morality should not be excessively demanding, but must allow each individual the moral liberty to act as she chooses so long as she does not wrongfully harm others, at least up to a point. Prioritarian axiology linked to act consequentialism upholds the togetherness of persons – each of us should always be promoting what would be impartially fair and good for all persons taken together. But anyway prioritarian axiology can be coupled with a deontological ethic with a beneficence duty less demanding than act consequentialism.

The slogan also suggests the idea that morality is in its essence a regulation of relations among separate persons – it dictates how one ought to relate to other persons and regard them, and is silent regarding how the individual relates to herself. Priority suggests otherwise – one is after all a person, and how one relates to oneself raises moral issues. Otsuka and Voorhoeve press yet another idea, the "unity of the self," namely that when considerations about how one person's condition compares to that of others are not in play, egalitarian norms including Pigou–Dalton are by the by, and trading off risk of harm for a person to gain a chance of a benefit for that very person so as to maximize her expected benefit is at least morally permissible. Priority on some construals disagrees, holding that in morality and in prudence, when facing risky prospects, we should choose in a way that is risk-averse with respect to lifetime individual well-being. Contemplating different ways in which one's own life might go can be relevantly like contemplating a choice between helping better-off Felicity or worse-off Dolores. One can have a duty of care, in a way, toward a worse-off possible future stage of oneself.

Response 1: Factualism

O and V see deficiency in priority emerging when one extends the ranking of outcomes to the ranking of possible outcomes, different ways in which the world might go. So any criterion of morally right action applied to that ranking of possible outcomes will go awry.

In response, Nils Holtug appeals to *factualism* (Holtug 2019). As an axiological doctrine, this says that priority is a rule for ranking outcomes not prospects. That is to say, morality tells us how to evaluate outcomes of what we might do given the actual empirical facts as they unfold. The chances that one's act might lead to one or another outcome is not germane to this outcome assessment and not relevant either to the further question, given the outcome an act produced, was it morally right or wrong. If morality dictates that it is wrong to kill someone for no good reason and handing my father this bottle would be killing him for no good reason, then according to factualism, it would be wrong to give my father the bottle. This is so even though nothing in the circumstances indicates that giving him the bottle would be killing him.

If we couple the prioritarian moral outcome ranking with an act consequentialist criterion of right action, the factualist sees the prioritarian criterion as identifying the morally right action, among the alternatives for choice, as any member of the set of actions that would actually bring about an outcome no worse than anything else one might instead have done, all other alternatives being wrong. Faced with a choice between an act that with probability p will bring about a very good outcome according to impartial assessment and with probability 1-p a very bad outcome, and another act, doing nothing, that will for sure bring about a middling outcome, the factualist will say one morally ought to do the risky act if and only if in fact it will lead to the very good outcome and not otherwise.

If we are seeking to formulate a criterion of morally right action, we should sharply distinguish this enterprise from the enterprise of developing a guide to agents for going about choosing one or another course of action. To the request for a decision-making guide, the factualist holds that one should choose in a way that is the best means to bringing about choice of actions that would be right by the factualist criterion. Here one should expect no theory, just pragmatic aids depending on one's circumstances.

Factualism provides a crisp clean response to the O and V objection that extends the priority criterion of choice to risky choice and criticizes this extension. The factualist denies the prioritarian is committed to any such extension and denies that any such extension is needed. In evaluating risky choices, our sole ultimate concern should be the moral value of the outcomes actually reached. In defense of this stance, one might insist that the only reason to be concerned with the expected value of the risky choices an agent might face is as a means to bringing about the best actual outcome. This instrumental concern should not color our view of what an agent morally ought to do.

In reply, a dissenter will insist we do have a moral concern to evaluate the choices people make with information available at the time of choice, a concern that does not reduce to outcome evaluation. It seems we do have and employ a notion answering to this concern. Suppose you feel sick and go to a medical doctor. Your physician examines you in what seems the normal professional manner, but he actually shakes dice to determine a diagnosis and treatment from an arbitrary list of alternatives. Suppose his prescribed medical treatment has a 99 percent chance of harming you and a one percent chance of doing you good. Alternative treatments that he overlooks would have a 99 percent chance of curing what ails you and a one percent chance of harming you. We already know enough to know that in a plain sense he has behaved wrongly, even though, if by a fluke his prescribed treatment does cure you, he has done what is right in the fact-relative sense. The factualist can say that the doctor in this case can be assessed as blameworthy even if doing no wrong, but even this may not be so. The doctor may have an extraordinary excuse for his wrongdoing, so not be blameworthy. Here the factualist cannot affirm a moral judgment of wrong conduct that needs to be made.

There is no deep puzzle or paradox here. We simply operate with two different and compatible ideas of the morally right (morally required) thing to do: as what it would be right to choose in the light of the available evidence at the time of choice, correctly interpreted, and alternatively, as what it would be right to do in the light of the actual facts of the situation as they turn out to be (Parfit 2011, 150–162). In the example in the previous paragraph, the physician does what is morally right in the fact-relative sense and what is morally wrong in the evidence-relative sense (in whatever plausible way we construe the latter). The two judgments are compatible and arguably our morality should yield both judgments about such cases.

The claim that we operate with two criteria of what it is morally right to do, a fact-relative and an evidence-relative idea, is fully compatible with the further claim that as practical guides to decision-making, individuals should employ whatever short cuts, cues, tricks, mnemonics, and norm adherence will enable them to come as close as possible to acting in conformity with theoretical criteria of morally right and wrong action.

But if there is a coherent, sensible conception of what it is morally right (required) to choose, when faced with a choice of actions, each of which will give rise to different outcomes depending on now uncertain future states of the world, we confront the Otsuka–Voorhoeve critique of the priority view. If a rival doctrine includes an appealing criterion of morally right action for risky choices, and priority cannot deliver an appealing evidence-relative criterion of what is morally right, that is a black mark against priority.

Response 2: Insulation

This pro-priority response, advanced by Matthew Adler (in Adler and Holtug, 2019), is in a way a close cousin of the Factualist response. The proposal is that as a matter of moral theory methodology, we ought to decide on questions of right and good as they would be seen by a fully informed deliberator. So we should consider the choice between sufficiency, priority, equality, utilitarian ranking, leximin, and perhaps other rivals, as axiological doctrines, by assessing how they rank for-sure outcomes. Having completed that assessment, we then consider proposed rules for ranking prospects, or lotteries with for-sure outcomes as prizes. Here we follow a two stage procedure. At the first stage we settle on a rule or standard for ranking for-sure outcomes, and at the second stage we confine our attention to proposals that are consistent with the already accepted rule for outcome ranking. Problems about how to rank very partially specified states of affairs characterized by poor information available to the assessor are cabined off from the task of identifying a correct outcome assessment standard. The best solution of the stage 2 task meets the condition that it is consistent with the best solution of the stage 1 task. Problems at stage 2 do not become reasons to reevaluate stage 1.

It is hard to be confident regarding the moral methodology norm that Adler suggests. Assume a background fallibilism. Any moral view we espouse, even the ones in which, in our present state of evidence and argument, we repose the fullest confidence, might turn out to be false, and reasonably rejectable in the light of further shifts in available evidence and argument. In that case, a problem in a remote corner of applied ethics might in principle unsettle any of our current views.

If priority appears so far as we can tell to be the winner of the stage 1 deliberation process, this fact provides some extra reason to search for a solution to stage 2 problems that does not require us to revisit and rethink stage 1. But it is hard to see why this should be a decisive consideration.

Response 3: Priority Is a Moral Principle That Does Not Apply to Decision Problems in Which Prudential Considerations Are All That Matter

Shlomi Segall (2015) has urged that prioritarianism is committed to treating intrapersonal tradeoffs and interpersonal tradeoffs on a par. The commitment stems from person separability (for risky choices, this becomes prospect separability). The doctrine will then require priority weighting in oneself-only choices. This invites the charge that priority is not properly responsive to the unity of the person and the separateness of persons. In a similar spirit Otsuka and Voorhoeve (2009, 2018; Otsuka 2015) object that in decision problems in which one is permitted to pay heed only to the interests of one person whom one seeks to help, priority (1) rules against choosing among prospects to maximize the expected utility of the person to be helped and (2) fails to treat differently cases in which different individuals have competing claims, and boosting one person's prospects comes at cost to others, from cases in which such competing claims are absent. The latter class of cases, besides the oneself-only ones already mentioned, includes those in which all those whose interests should be considered face prospects that move in lockstep across whatever choices one could make.

It is perhaps unclear how best to extend priority rankings of for-sure outcomes to rankings of prospects. But the most prominent and accepted such extension is ex post priority-weighted maximization. This ex post priority rule for assessing prospects definitely conflicts with ex ante EU assessment. Conforming to the first will sometime require failing to conform to the second. But EU has great virtues, so this conflict is a great theoretical cost that must be borne by the priority advocate.

The response alleges that this problem is spurious. The key is to notice that "morality is a framework for resolving interpersonal conflicts; but in a one-person universe there are no such conflicts" (Adler and Holtug 2019, 121). People's interests often conflict. My avoiding the onerous labor of shoveling the snow from my walk may be in conflict with your need for safe passage along my walk without falling and injuring yourself and without suffering excessive delay as you trundle along. Morality by definition of the term has as its aim the identification of principles and procedures that fairly and appropriately settle such conflicts. A candidate morality that leaves conflicts of interest theoretically unresolved is not completely fulfilling its conceptual role. Or one might alternatively stipulate that morality conceptually involves the determination what to do in decision problems in which several persons' interests are involved so that there could conceivably be conflicts of interest (even if sometimes there are no actual conflicts of interests among persons in the decision problem one faces).

So understood, the recommendations as to what one ought to do propounded by moral theories or sets of moral principles and the recommendations as to what one ought to do propounded by theories of rational prudence can differ, and tell the agent to do opposed and conflicting acts, without contradicting each other. A theory of prudence says what choices of action by an individual would be most to that individual's advantage. Against a backdrop in which it is assumed that each individual has interests, satisfying which will make her life go better for that very individual, prudence is the norm that tells each of us that she should choose and do whatever actions would be best for her, in the sense of maximizing her advantage level or the satisfaction of her own interests. Morality might specify that I ought to shovel my walk when it snows and prudence might dictate that in the same circumstances I ought to refrain from shoveling my walk.

But in oneself-only decision problems, in which no one's interests are affected but those of the individual agent who is choosing an action, morality is silent, for in such situations there is no conflict of interest among persons.

If ex post priority-weighted welfare maximization is a moral principle, it is silent in oneself-only choices. So nothing bars the prioritarian from accepting EU as the norm that governs what one ought to do in oneself-only risky decision problems, and also in situations in which there are several individuals, all of whose prospects rise and fall together so that the decision problem is like several oneself-only problems stacked together. In this range of cases at least the conflict between prioritarian moral outcome assessment and prudential EU outcome assessment dissolves. The prioritarian moralist can accept EU as the right norm for prospect evaluation on its home ground. So runs response #3.

However, the conceptual point about what morality fundamentally is does not rule out the possibility that the principles that finally come to emerge in extended reflective equilibrium as the right rules for resolving interpersonal conflicts of interest might turn out to have implications for other sorts of decision problems. Reasons go where they go; there are no limits in principle to their reach. In particular, it could turn out to be the case that the principles that answer to the moral issue of what we owe one another in the face of conflicts of interest among persons also tell us what to do in cases where what the agent chooses can have an impact on the welfare only of that very agent.

Something like this turns out to be the case with utilitarianism. What holds for utilitarianism also holds, on its face, for prioritarianism. The rule that we are to evaluate outcomes by the total sum of well-being they contain, summed across individuals, does not cease to apply when the set of individuals is a singleton, and the same with the rule, the greater the priority-weighted sum of well-being, the better the outcome. Of course, such a claim is not self-certifying. But it merits a response.

Response 4: Priority Applies to Oneself-Only Decision Problems, and Rightly So. Prudence and Morality Here Conflict

It is not mysterious that prudence and morality can conflict in situations in which people's interests conflict. The best prospect for me may arise from my grabbing all the marbles for myself whereas the moral choice would require choosing the act with the best prospect of sharing the marbles fairly among all who might be affected.

Response #4 maintains that prudent assessment and moral assessment of prospects can conflict even in situations in which only one person may be affected in the outcome or in which the several persons who may be affected will be affected identically in welfare gain or loss, whatever action is chosen (Rabinowicz 2002; see also O'Neill 2012). In these cases, moral assessment of prospects requires ranking them by the sum of priority-weighted well-being they contain; prudent assessment requires ranking prospects by their expected well-being. From the two perspectives the verdicts about what to do in the face of risk differ but are not contradictory; it can be true both that morality requires one, say, to decline the gamble on offer and prudence to accept it. What we should do all things considered would be a further question; the prioritarian moralist can, but need not, hold that morality is the supreme practical reason ruler.

This response preserves prioritarian morality from objections based on its coming into conflict with the decision theory norm that rationality requires maximizing expected value.

Response 5: Priority Applies to Oneself-Only Decision Problems, and Rightly So. Here Prudence and Morality Cannot Conflict, So Priority for Prospects Is Required by Prudence

The last response zigs where response #4 zags (see Porter 2012 and Crisp 2012). In decision problems in which no one could be affected but yourself, prudence says, do what would be best for yourself, and with risky choices, expectably best. In decision problems in which no one could be affected but yourself, utilitarian morality says, do what would be best for yourself, and with risky choices, expectably best. How could prudence and morality conflict in such cases?

One possible wedge separating prudence and morality in oneself-only choices arises from the idea that morality favors, to some degree, welfare gains for persons over same-sized welfare gains for nonpersons, given that one might face tradeoffs between obtaining a smaller gain now or instead a larger gain for a future demented stage of oneself. Accepting this, we might still with plausibility maintain, in cases in which all that matters for a choice is its future effect on my own well-being during stages of my life when I will for sure remain a full person, the verdicts of morality as to what I should do and the verdicts of prudence must coincide, cannot conflict.

If we accept, with response #4, that the moral evaluation of prospects must be adjusted to reflect ex post priority for the worse off, then we should accept the further idea, that the evaluation of prospects from the prudential standpoint must also and equally be adjusted in the exact same way. To put the conclusion starkly, a rationally prudent person facing risky gambling choices is risk-averse in terms of the well-being outcomes that may befall her, where "well-being" refers to whatever would in itself make her life go best for her. In fact, priority requires not just some risk aversion but a specific magnitude, or at least a delimited acceptable range, and this priority-weighted magnitude constrains both acceptable prudent choice between possible futures for oneself and acceptable moral tradeoffs of the interests of better-off and worse-off persons (Broome 1991 interprets prioritarianism this way, rejecting the doctrine so interpreted). What is expectably best for a person deviates across the board from the dictates of standard expected utility theory.

This position may be correct despite its being controversial. Standard decision theory is permissive, requiring only that an agent's beliefs, preferences and choices of action be coherent (or that one's acts effectively advance the satisfaction of one's preferences given one's beliefs). Some alternative normative decision theory proposals enhance this permissiveness, allowing that being risk-averse in utility or risk-seeking or risk-neutral can be coherent (Buchak 2013). This idea of rationality has important uses. It leaves open the possibility that another notion of rationality might be more substantially constraining, denying for example that preferring pain over pleasure can be substantially rational, and if the prioritarian is right, denying that refraining from favoring worse offs over better offs can be morally acceptable, and adding that neither can refraining from favoring possible worse-off over better-off future stages of oneself be prudentially acceptable. Of course this substantial account will look arbitrarily dogmatic from the permissive perspective.

One might object that priority in effect treats possible future alternative continuations of oneself as owed fair distribution just as possible alternative distributions across actual persons raise distributive fairness issues. But consider choices one can make that might bring about the existence of future persons at varying well-being levels. These possible future persons may never become actual, yet their interests can affect what one has good reason to do. The same goes with possible continuations of oneself, and what one may owe to them is preventing their becoming actual or reducing the chances they will become actual.

Consider a clear example of a oneself-only risky decision problem. Robinson alone on his island can affect no one's interests but his own in the choices he makes. Let him be the sole person who ever exists in the universe. Suppose he faces a choice with a possible decisive impact on his overall lifetime well-being. He could choose either one of just two options: swim with the sharks (fun, but risks death or disablement) or play on the sand (boring but safe). For simplicity, suppose this choice fixes his lifetime well-being. The remainder of his life will be a solid block, with all his choices already determined. The relevant states of nature affecting the outcomes are S1 overcast sky (enabling sharks to bite) or S2 sunny (these imaginary sharks lack ability to smell prey and must rely on their weak vision, which sunshine occludes, so no sharkbite). The probability of S1 is five percent and of S2, 95 percent. Sunny or overcast sky does not affect the payoff from playing on the sand. The payoffs for Robinson in lifetime well-being are as follows:

Prospect #1 (Swim with sharks)		Prospect #2 (Play on sand)	
S1	S2	S1	S2
10	200	190	190

The expected well-being of swimming with the sharks is higher than the expected well-being of playing on the sand, but we can suppose the probability-weighted ex post priority-weighted well-being of the latter choice is higher. Priority weighting requires that Robinson be risk-averse in well-being in evaluating risky prospects. Priority as we are interpreting it here requires that Robinson give extra weight to avoiding low lifetime well-being options in intrapersonal choice, exactly as he would be required to give extra weight to avoiding low lifetime well-being outcomes in risky choice involving interpersonal conflict of interest. Thinking of his possible futures, he should care more for helping the possible future extension of himself that dies tragically young than for the extension that lives long and happy, just as he should care more for Dolores the homeless waif than for Felicity the fulfilled entrepreneur in the Section 1 example we used to introduce the priority idea.

The requirement of risk aversion in well-being prospects when no one is affected by the agent herself can seem arbitrarily restrictive. Why can't I take a gamble, even a poor gamble, at least when only I am affected?

But here we should distinguish axiology and act evaluation. Accepting prioritarian outcome evaluation leaves open the question, what principles determine the moral permissibility of acts. Coupling prioritarian axiology with act consequentialism yields the verdict that one must do what maximizes priority-weighted well-being, and the natural extension to risky choice yields the judgment that one must maximize probability-weighted ex post priority-weighted well-being. But accepting prioritarian axiology leaves open adopting a deontological ethic that says, for example, each person is morally permitted to act as she chooses when no else is adversely affected. That's as may be. But this respect for autonomy, if acceptable, would license expected utility maximizing in decision problems involving interpersonal as well as intrapersonal tradeoffs, as when a bunch of people agree together to a set of gambles that will definitely leave some far better off than others ex post. If morality includes a beneficence requirement that is keyed to increasing priority-weighted well-being, then the more that this requirement looms large as a component of moral requirements, the greater the role that priority-weighted evaluation of risky prospects plays in determining what all things considered morality requires one to do.

One should also note that ex post well-being prioritarianism does not rule out risk-taking in ordinary life. Being risk-averse with respect to well-being is compatible with being risk-neutral or risk-seeking in other terms such as money or health. Depending on the numbers, ex post well-being prioritarianism might recommend to Robinson in many situations that he swim with the sharks, to Sally that she become a riverboat gambler or venture capitalist, to Tamara that she go in for extreme sports. That depends on the priority-weighted expected value of the available alternatives. Priority simply says, avoiding a given loss in well-being has increasing moral value, the worse of one otherwise is, and on the extension considered here, prospects should also be evaluated via priority weighting.

This solution of the puzzle that Otuska and Voorhoeve press against the prioritarian has the advantage of avoiding having to say that prudence and welfarist morality may conflict when no one's interests can be affected by one's choice except one's own. The disadvantage is that this solution conflicts flatly with normative expected utility theory (EU), and rejecting EU according to the received view requires giving up one or another uncontroversially binding condition on rational choice. Unless some fancy revision of EU can avoid or soften this implication, we seem to be in a bind. (Exploring the relevant decision theory goes beyond what can be attempted in this short introduction to the prioritarianism topic.)

6 Conclusion

If any of these responses or some combination of them is successful, priority withstands the recent egalitarian critique. I have given considerable space in this Element to equality versus priority. In the vast landscape of moral doctrines, priority and equality by any reasonable similarity metric are similar views, so their disagreement has something of the interest of a quarrel among closely related family members. But interest may not correlate with moral importance. As mentioned already, priority and equality will in many circumstances be close comrades fighting on the same side of the barricades against familiar broadly nonegalitarian common foes.

References

Adler, M., *Well-being and Fair Distribution: Beyond Cost-Benefit Analysis*, Oxford, Oxford University Press, 2012.

Adler, M., "Prioritarianism: Room for Desert?" *Utilitas* 30 (2018), 172–197.

Adler, M., and Holtug, N., "Prioritarianism: A Response to Critics," *Politics, Philosophy, and Economics* 18 (2019), 101–144.

Arneson, R., "Desert and Equality," in N. Holtug and K. Lippert-Rasmussen, eds., *Egalitarianism: New Essays on the Nature and Value of Equality*, Oxford, Oxford University Press, 2007, 262–293.

Arneson, R., "Individual Well-Being and Social Justice," *Proceedings and Addresses of the American Philosophical Association* 93 (2019), 39–66.

Arpaly, N., "Moral Worth," *Journal of Philosophy* 99 (2002), 223–245.

Benbaji, Y., "The Doctrine of Sufficiency: A Defense," *Utilitas* 17 (2005), 310–332.

Benbaji, Y., "Sufficiency or Priority?" *European Journal of Philosophy* 14 (2006), 327–348.

Bradley, R., *Decision Theory with a Human Face*, Cambridge, Cambridge University Press, 2017.

Broome, J., *Weighing Goods: Equality, Uncertainty, and Time*, Oxford, Blackwell's, 1991.

Broome, J., "Equality and Priority: A Useful Distinction," *Economics and Philosophy* 31 (2015), 219–228.

Buchak, L., *Risk and Rationality*, Oxford, Oxford University Press, 2013.

Buchak, L., "Taking Risks Behind the Veil of Ignorance," *Ethics* 127 (2017), 610–644.

Bykvist, K., "Utilitarianism in the Twentieth Century," in B. Eggleston and D. Miller, eds., *The Cambridge Companion to Utilitarianism*, Cambridge, Cambridge University Press, 2014, 103-124.

Casal, P., "Why Sufficiency Is Not Enough," *Ethics* 117 (2007), 296–326.

Crisp, R., "Equality, Priority, and Compassion," *Ethics* 113 (2003), 745–763.

Crisp, R., "In Defense of the Priority View: A Response to Otsuka and Voorhoeve," *Utilitas* 23 (2011), 105–108.

Diamond, P., "Cardinal Welfare, Individualistic Ethics, and Interpersonal Comparisons of Utility: Comment," *Journal of Political Economy* 75 (1967), 765–766.

Dworkin, R., *Sovereign Virtue: The Theory and Practice of Equality*, Cambridge, MA, Harvard University Press, 2000.

Eyal, N., "Egalitarian Justice and Innocent Choice," *Journal of Ethics and Social Philosophy* 2 (2007), 1–18.

Feldman, F., "Adjusting Utility for Justice: A Consequentialist Reply to the Objection from Justice," *Philosophy and Phenomenological Research*, 55 (1995), 567–585.

Feldman, F., *Distributive Justice: Getting What We Deserve from Our Country*, Oxford, Oxford University Press, 2016.

Fleurbaey, M., "Assessing Risky Social Situations," *Journal of Political Economy* 118 (2010), 649–680.

Fleurbaey, M., "Equality Versus Priority: How Relevant Is the Distinction?" *Economics and Philosophy* 31 (2015), 203–217.

Fleurbaey, M., and Voorhoeve, A., "Egalitarianism and the Separateness of Persons," *Utilitas* 24 (2012), 381–398.

Frankfurt, H., "Equality as a Moral Ideal," in H. Frankfurt, ed., *The Importance of What We Care About*, Cambridge, Cambridge University Press, 1998, 134-158.

Greaves, H., "A Reconsideration of the Harsanyi-Sen-Weymark Debate on Utilitarianism," *Utilitas* 29 (2016), 175–213.

Harsanyi, J., "Cardinal Utility in Welfare Economics and in the Theory of Risk-Taking," *Journal of Political Economy*, 61 (1953), 434–435.

Harsanyi, J., "Cardinal Welfare, Individualistic Ethics, and Interpersonal Comparisons of Utility," *Journal of Political Economy* 63 (1955), 309–321.

Hirose, I., *Egalitarianism*, London, Routledge, 2015, Chapters 4 and 5.

Holtug, N., "On Giving Priority to Possible Future People, in T. Rannow-Rasmussen, et al., eds., *Hommage a Wlodek: Philosophical Papers Dedicated to Wlodek Rabinowicz*, 2007, www.fil.lu.se/hommageawlodek

Holtug, N., *Persons, Interests, and Justice*, Oxford, Oxford University Press, 2010.

Holtug, N., "Prioritarianism: Ex Ante, Ex Post, or Factualist Criterion of Right?" *Journal of Political Philosophy* 27 (2019), 207–228.

Kagan, S., *The Geometry of Desert*, Oxford, Oxford University Press, 2012.

Kavka, G., "Some Paradoxes of Deterrence," *Journal of Philosophy* 75 (1978), 285–302.

McKerkie, D., "Dimensions of Egalitarianism," *Utilitas* 13 (2001), 263–288.

McKerlie, D., *Justice between the Young and the Old*, Oxford, Oxford University Press, 2013.

Mill, J. S., *Utilitarianism*, ed. G. Sher, Indianapolis, Hackett, 1979. Originally published 1861.

Moriarty, J., "Desert-based Justice," in S. Olsaretti, ed., *The Oxford Handbook of Distributive Justice*, Oxford, Oxford University Press, 2018, 152–173.

Nagel, T, "Equality," in T. Nagel, ed., *Mortal Questions*, Cambridge, Cambridge University Press, 1979, 106–127.

Nozick, R., *Anarchy, State, and Utopia*, New York, Basic Books, 1974.

O'Neill, M., "Priority, Preference, and Value," *Utilitas* 24 (2012), 332–348.

Otsuka, M., "Prioritarianism and the Measure of Utility," *Journal of Political Philosophy* 23 (2015), 1–22.

Otsuka, M., and Voorhoeve, A., "Why It Matters that Some Are Worse Off than Others: An Argument against the Priority View," *Philosophy and Public Affairs* 37 (2009), 171–199.

Otsuka, M., and Voorhoeve, A., "Equality versus Priority," in S. Olsaretti, ed., *The Oxford Handbook of Distributive Justice*, Oxford, Oxford University Press, 2018, 65–85.

Parfit, D., "Equality or Priority?" *The Lindley Lecture*, University of Kansas, 1995.

Parfit, D., *On What Matters*, vol. 1, Oxford, Oxford University Press, 2011.

Parfit, D., "Another Defense of the Priority *View*," *Utilitas* 24 (2012), 399–440.

Pereboom, D., *Living without Free Will*, Cambridge, Cambridge University Press, 2001.

Porter, T., "In Defence of the Priority View," *Utilitas* 24 (2012), 349–364.

Rabinowicz, W., "Prioritarianism for Prospects," *Utilitas* 14 (2002), 2–21.

Rae, D. et al., *Inequalities*, Cambridge, Harvard University Press, 1981.

Rawls, J., *A Theory of Justice*, rev. ed., Cambridge, MA, Harvard University Press, 1999.

Risse, M., "Harsanyi's 'Utilitarian Theorem' and Utilitarianism," *Nous* 36 (2002), 550–557.

Risse, M., *On Global Justice*, Princeton and Oxford, Princeton University Press, 2012.

Roemer, J., *Theories of Distributive Justice*, Cambridge, MA, Harvard University Press, Chapter 4, 1996.

Roemer, J., "Egalitarianism against the Veil of Ignorance," *Journal of Philosophy* 99 (2002), 167–184.

Ross, W. D., *The Right and the Good*, Oxford, Oxford University Press, 1930.

Scanlon, T. M., "Rawls on Justification," in S. Freeman, ed., *The Cambridge Companion to Rawls*, Cambridge, Cambridge University Press, 2003, 139–167.

Segall, S., "In Defense of Priority (and Equality)," *Politics, Philosophy, and Economics*, 14 (2015), 343–364.

Sen, A., "Welfare Inequalities and Rawlsian Axiomatics," *Theory and Decision* 7 (1975), 243–262.

Sumner, L. W., *Welfare, Happiness, and Ethics*, Oxford, Oxford University Press, 1996.

Tadros, V., *Wrongs and Crimes*, Oxford, Oxford University Press, 2016.

Temkin, L., *Inequality*, Oxford, Oxford University Press, 1993.

Temkin, L., "Inequality: A Complex, Individualistic, and Comparative Notion," *Philosophical Issues* 11 (2001), 327–353.

Vallentyne, P., "Of Mice and Men: Equality and Animals," *Journal of Ethics* 9 (2005), 403–433.

Vallentyne, P., "Critical Notice of Matthew D. Adler's *Well-Being and Fair Distribution,*" *Analysis Reviews* 1 (2013), 1–7.

Weber, M., "Prioritarianism," *Philosophy Compass* 9 (2014), 315–331.

Weirich, P., "Utility Tempered with Equality," *Nous* 17 (1983), 315–331.

Weymark, J., "A Reconsideration of the Harsanyi-Sen Debate on Utilitarianism," in J. Elster and J. Roemer, eds., *Interpersonal Comparisons of Well-Being*, Cambridge, Cambridge University Press, 1991, 255–320.

Weymark, J., "Measurement Theory and the Foundations of Utilitarianism," *Social Choice and Welfare*, 25 (2005), 527–555.

Williams, A., "The Priority View Bites the Dust?" *Utilitas* 24 (2012), 315–331.

Ethics

Ben Eggleston

University of Kansas

Ben Eggleston is a professor of philosophy at the University of Kansas. He is the editor of John Stuart Mill, *Utilitarianism: With Related Remarks from Mill's Other Writings* (Hackett, 2017) and a co-editor of *Moral Theory and Climate Change: Ethical Perspectives on a Warming Planet* (Routledge, 2020), *The Cambridge Companion to Utilitarianism* (Cambridge, 2014), and *John Stuart Mill and the Art of Life* (Oxford, 2011). He is also the author of numerous articles and book chapters on various topics in ethics.

Dale E. Miller

Old Dominion University, Virginia

Dale E. Miller is a professor of philosophy at Old Dominion University. He is the author of *John Stuart Mill: Moral, Social and Political Thought* (Polity, 2010) and a co-editor of *Moral Theory and Climate Change: Ethical Perspectives on a Warming Planet* (Routledge, 2020), *A Companion to Mill* (Blackwell, 2017), *The Cambridge Companion to Utilitarianism* (Cambridge, 2014), *John Stuart Mill and the Art of Life* (Oxford, 2011), and *Morality, Rules, and Consequences: A Critical Reader* (Edinburgh, 2000). He is also the editor-in-chief of *Utilitas*, and the author of numerous articles and book chapters on various topics in ethics broadly construed.

About the Series

This Elements series provides an extensive overview of major figures, theories, and concepts in the field of ethics. Each entry in the series acquaints students with the main aspects of its topic while articulating the author's distinctive viewpoint in a manner that will interest researchers.

Cambridge Elements ⁼

Ethics

Elements in the Series

Morality and Practical Reasons
Douglas W. Portmore

Subjective versus Objective Moral Wrongness
Peter A. Graham

Parfit's Ethics
Richard Yetter Chappell

Moral Psychology
Christian B. Miller

Philippa Foot's Metaethics
John Hacker-Wright

Natural Law Theory
Tom Angier

Happiness and Well-Being
Chris Heathwood

Ethical Constructivism
Carla Bagnoli

Hume on the Nature of Morality
Elizabeth S. Radcliffe

Kant's Ethics
Kate A. Moran

Ethical Realism
William J. FitzPatrick

Prioritarianism
Richard J. Arneson

A full series listing is available at www.cambridge.org/EETH

Printed in the United States
by Baker & Taylor Publisher Services